So, you've made it three months. Congratulations! This is where the fun really begins. What a thrill when your baby begins to coo to you or smile when you appear at her crib and you realize she's becoming a real little person. Soon your baby will laugh right out loud. Many of the following games were designed to encourage laughing, by tickling, kissing or surprising an unsuspecting baby! So, come on and have a few laughs.

Bed Bouncies

Purpose: To encourage the baby to laugh; to develop balance.

Equipment: A double bed is best, but a single will do.

Position: Place the baby on her back on the bed and lean over her with your palms flat on the top of the bed on either side of her head, or at chest height.

Procedure: 1. With your hands, give the bed a series of little bounces—not too hard at first.

GAMES BABIES PLAY & MORE GAMES BABIES PLAY

**JULIE HAGSTROM
& JOAN MORRILL**

*Illustrations by
Christiane Stalland*

PUBLISHED BY POCKET BOOKS NEW YORK

POCKET BOOKS, a division of Simon & Schuster, Inc.
1230 Avenue of the Americas, New York, N.Y. 10020

Copyright © 1979 by Joan Morrill and Julie Hagstrom
Copyright © 1981 by Julie Hagstrom

Published by arrangement with A&W Publishers, Inc.
Library of Congress Catalog Card Number:

Games Babies Play 78-70684
More Games Babies Play 80-66264

ISBN: 0-671-49888-6

First Pocket Books printing September, 1981

10 9 8 7 6 5 4 3 2

POCKET and colophon are registered trademarks
of Simon & Schuster, Inc.

Printed in the U.S.A.

Book I

GAMES
BABIES
PLAY

*A Handbook of Games
to Play with Infants*

For Jerry, who played the
games with Amy, and
to Amy, with love.

Contents

Preface

This book has been developed from the experiences my husband and I shared with Amy, our first child. Her arrival was anticipated and planned for with much fuss and excitement, and when the three of us came home from the hospital, we hoped to find a routine that would be compatible with our way of life.

Actually, we found abundant advice from all sides of the family. There were as many philosophies as there were visitors, ranging from "Never let her cry!" to "Let her cry thirty minutes—she'll learn her schedule!" There were many suggestions about rocking and/or walking with her, pacifiers (pro and con), bottles, and oh, yes—a biggie—burping, how and when.

To be honest, since we were new at this, much of the advice was useful and truly appreciated; but each family has to find the techniques and routines with which it feels most comfortable. New parents often find it hard to assert their authority over the old-timers. Luckily, Jerry, my husband, did not. This book began when Amy was several days old, had just been fed, and was being held by Jerry. My mother said, "Well, aren't you going to put her to bed?" Jerry firmly replied, "There's more to life than eating and sleeping, Joan."

He was right. And my mother agreed as she saw our daily routine develop to include food, sleep, bath, *and* play. Slowly and naturally, out of our love for Amy and our desire to be with her and hold her, came a whole series of structured games, stretching from birth to her first birthday—games babies play.

I would like to thank the following babies for postponing naps and rushing through bottles and baths in order to play some of these games with me: Jennifer Shaw, Devon Straitiff, Shane Milne, Megan Cocking.

Thanks also to my older players, Barbie and Kimmy Wayne.

—J. H., 1978

Foreword

I am Joan Morrill, and this is a sketch of my granddaughter, Amy Hagstrom. I'll tell you what is happening here. I am baby-sitting, and Amy is trying to teach me a game she knows. Her father taught *her*, but he didn't teach me! When Julie and Jerry came home, I said, "I need a rule book so I can play Amy's games." So Julie told me how, and now I am telling you—how to have more fun than ever with babies.

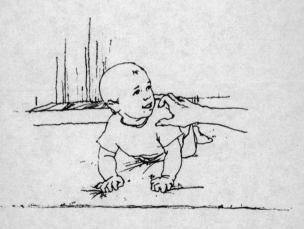

PART 1

Birth to Six Weeks

Stimulation Games

When teaching games to a new baby, you will have to be the active participant, playing the games *for* her more than with her.* These first six weeks are a crucial time for baby because you are building her confidence in you and in life itself; also, you are preparing her for games to come in which she can actively participate. By playing with your baby, you become better acquainted with her feelings, likes, and dislikes. And what better way is there to learn about another person than to play games together?

The first game in this section is designed to relax both baby and her parents. (A relaxed baby sleeps and eats well; this helps the adult who is caring for the infant, too!) The next two games will stimulate the baby's interest in herself, you, and other people. The last game stimulates her sense of rhythm.

---

*No offense, please, players with boy-baby partners, but we are going to stick to "her" throughout this book.

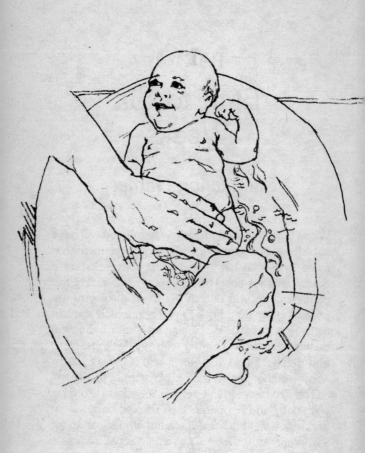

1
Pat-the-baby

Purpose: To relax tense muscles
To become aware of body

Equipment: None

Position: Lay the baby on her back on a quilt. Sit or kneel beside her.

Procedure:
1. Gently *stroke* the baby's arms, from shoulders to hands. Stroke her legs, from hips to feet. While stroking, speak softly or sing quietly.
2. Extend the baby's arms, and *pat* one arm at a time (with a hand on either side of the arm), from shoulder to fingertips. Do the same to the legs. Repeat several times.
3. Gently *stroke* under the baby's chin in a half-circle motion. Stroke the side of the baby's head from the top of the forehead, down past the temples, in front of the ears, to beneath the chin.
4. *Rub* the baby's hands and feet between your own hands.

Variations:	Hold the baby on your shoulder, supporting her firmly, and rub her back and the back of her head.
Suggestions:	Play this game with the baby just before her bath or nap. The baby may like a quick round of Pat-the-baby after her bath. Don't play for more than ten minutes at a time.

2
You and Me, Baby!

Purpose: To help the baby become aware of similarities between herself and others

Equipment: None

Position: Put the baby on her back on a quilt on the floor. Kneel above the baby.

Procedure: 1. Lower your face close to the baby's, and gently guide the baby's hands over your face, quietly naming the features of the face. Repeat this several times.

2. Gently guide the baby's hands over your hands. Repeat twice.

Variations: Hold the baby on your lap. Let another player guide her hands. Also, you can guide the baby's hands over her own face, remembering always to name the features.

3

Follow the Face

Purpose	To stimulate the baby's visual perception
	To encourage her to follow moving objects with her eyes
Equipment	Brightly colored puppet, or a doll with a face
Position:	Place the baby on her back on a quilt on the floor or in her bassinet. Sit facing the baby at eye level.

Procedure: 1. Begin by leaning your face close to the baby's. Move your head from side to side, softly calling the baby's name: "Amy, look at Grandma." Watch to see if the baby's eyes are following your face. Repeat this step for a few minutes.

   2. Lie down beside the baby, and hold a brightly colored doll or puppet so that its face is above the baby's. Wiggle the doll to get the baby's attention. Then, talk for the doll: "Hi, Amy! My name is Susy. Watch me!" Slowly move the doll from side to side, watching to see if the baby's eyes follow it. Repeat for three or four minutes.

Suggestions: Be sure to lie down for this game. If you sit above the baby, she may watch you instead of the doll or puppet. Also, since studies have shown that babies prefer three-dimensional faces to pictures of faces or plain bright colors, it is important that the toy have a face (newborn infants, however, respond well to bright, linear patterns).

4
Dance with Me

Purpose: To help the baby recognize her own sense of rhythm, which will serve as a basis for future skills

Equipment: Lively, but simple tune—record, tape, or live

Position: Stand up, holding the baby firmly against your chest with one hand holding the baby's head against your shoul-

der, and the other hand supporting the rest of the baby's body.

Procedure: Begin the music, and sway gently back and forth, humming the tune or singing the words softly to the baby.

Variations: Hold the baby as in the picture above. While sitting, hold baby parallel to the floor, cradling her head in your hands. In this position, you can see baby's face and make eye contact. Rock gently back and forth.

Suggestions: Play Dance with Me all through baby's first year. (See Game 22, page 68.)

PART 2

Six to Twelve Weeks

Reaction Games

By this time, Amy was actively participating in our games together. She was reacting to her world with a personality and sense of humor all her own. A baby will begin to smile and coo during this period; and music boxes, brightly colored mobiles, and jungle gyms provide a source of entertainment when you're not around to play games.

The pediatrician gave us the go-ahead to take Amy to the beach, as long as she was kept out of the sun and we used a protective sun-guard lotion. This opened a whole new world of stimuli to which Amy could react: waves breaking, people laughing and shouting, birds crying above, the smell of sea spray, and the sight and touch (not to mention the taste!) of hot sand, wet sand, and salt water.

And after a vigorous two-hour session at the beach, a bath and a relaxing round of Pat-the-baby or a quiet Dance with Me often helped Amy cope with any overstimulation.

5

Mirror, Mirror

Purpose: To develop self-awareness

Equipment: Large, fixed mirror; small mirror with handle

Position: Hold the baby in your arms, both of you facing the mirror.

Procedure: Smile at the baby. Name the baby and yourself: "There's Amy. There's Grandma." Touch the mirror. Take the baby's hand and touch the mirror.

Variations:
1. Make a happy face. Say, "See the happy face."
2. Make a sad face. Say, "See the sad face."
3. Let the baby hold the mirror and look at herself.
4. Place the baby's hand on the mirror so she can touch the reflection of her own hand.

6
Mousie

Purpose: To develop a sense of humor by encouraging the giggles

Equipment: None

Position: Hold the baby on your lap, or play with her while she is in an infant seat or lying on her stomach on the floor.

Procedure: Make your fingers travel up the baby's legs in a creeping motion, saying, "Creepie, creepie, little mousie." Starting up the arm, say, " . . . right into your little . . ." Just as you reach the back of the baby's neck, say, "housie!" (Not too loud on the "housie!") Give the baby a little tickle and a big hug. Very repeatable.

Suggestion: A baby who's unhappy in her car seat is liable to perk up as the mousie steals slowly up her legs.

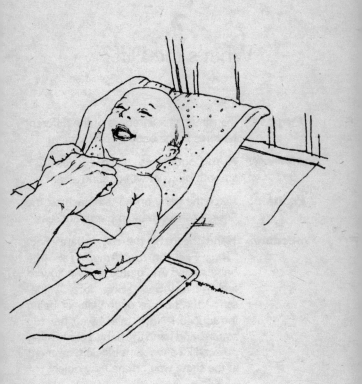

7
What's the Diff?

Purpose: To stimulate awareness of the different textures in the baby's environment

Equipment: A rug square, a piece of velvet, a smooth block of wood, sand

Position: Place the baby on her stomach on the floor, or she can be in her infant seat.

Procedure: Hand the baby the rug square. Say, "Rug. Feel the rug, Amy." Take the baby's hand and gently show it how to feel the rug. Say, "Soft, fuzzy." (Describe the texture of the object being introduced.) Now, take away the rug square, and hand the baby a contrasting object, like a wooden block. Comment in the same way on the new object.

Variation: Put the baby in a position to play the game by herself. That is, lay her on her stomach on a rug that is touching clean linoleum. Take the baby's hand and put it on the two surfaces, alternately, saying, "Soft, fuzzy" and "Hard, smooth."

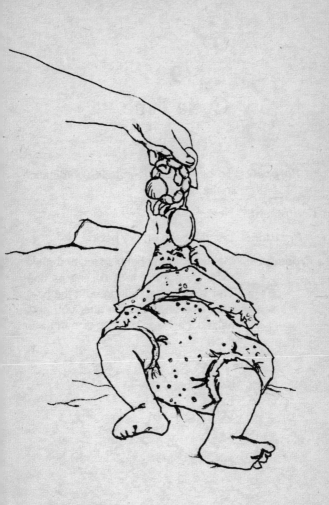

9

Cycle Time

Purpose: To develop large-muscle coordination in the baby's legs

Equipment: None

Position: Lay the baby on her back.

Procedure: Gently hold the baby's feet, and make them go around in a cycling motion. This is a natural motion, and the baby will carry on the game after you have helped her "rev up" for a minute or two!

PART 3

Three to Six Months

Games of Suspense

Now is the time to get some colorful, chewable, noise toys so baby can entertain herself. After all, grown-ups can't be playing games all the time! This is when the Jolly Jump-Up or a walker comes in handy; Amy enjoyed having the world at her feet, for a change! Don't forget, one of a baby's favorite ways of entertaining herself while everyone's busy is to play with her feet!

A backpack baby carrier can open up a whole new travel style. This is the only way to go to shopping centers or on rustic walks.

Now that the beds are made and the laundry started, let's play a game. We all love Hide-and-go-seek, ghost stories, roller coasters (well, most of us); so why not let the baby fulfill her instinctive pleasure in the unexpected? We can help her accept surprise with happiness and security, rather than with fear. Come on, let's have some scary fun!

10
Peek-a-boo

Purpose: Peek-a-boo is like Hide-and-go-seek—it has an element of surprise and is just a little bit scary! It is played for fun.

Equipment: Use your hands or a book or the baby's towel-hood.

Position: Put the baby in an infant seat. Sit in front of the baby.

Procedure: Put your hands in front of your face. Say, "Where's Grandma?" Wait about five seconds. Take your hands away, and say, "Peek-a-boo!" Got it? Repeat this at least ten times, until the baby gets the joke.

Variations: 1. After her bath, cover baby's head with a corner of her towel. Count to three. Say, "Where's Amy?" Flip the corner back. Say, "Peek-a-boo!" Give her a hug. Scary games should always be softened with hugs.

2. You can crouch down below the crib when the baby is playing in it.

39

Say, in a spooky voice, "Where's Mama?" Then pop your head up and say (you guessed it), "Peek-a-boo!" Or, cover the head of the baby's doll. Say, "Where's dolly?" Flip the handkerchief (or diaper) off. Have the dolly say, "Peek-a-boo!"

Suggestion: Be sure to wait only a few seconds between asking, "Where's . . .?" and saying, "Peek-a-boo." Most babies will lose interest (if they are the peek-a-boo-er) or become frightened (if they are the peek-a-boo-ee) if you wait too long between steps.

11
Gotcha!

Purpose: To develop a sense of timing in the baby as she anticipates how the game will continue

Equipment: None

Position: Sit the baby on the floor if she has learned to sit; otherwise, place her on her back on the floor. Sit facing the baby, or lean over her if she is on her back.

Procedure:
1. Smiling, slowly come closer to the baby with hands outstretched. Say softly, "I'm going to get you! Look out, Amy! Here I come . . ."
2. As you come close to the baby, gently grab her, while you say, "Gotcha!" in a louder voice than at first, but not shouting.
3. Laugh and hug the baby after each "Gotcha!" to let the baby know it's a game.
4. Repeat five to ten times, so the baby can get used to the game and begin

to anticipate the exciting ending as you are about to "zero in."

Variations: A reluctant Gotcha! player may enjoy having one adult player hold her while another player slowly comes forward to administer the "Gotcha!" This way, the baby can hug and be hugged, feeling safe the whole time. Also, if the baby is sitting up by herself, you can circle around to the back of her, calling softly, "I'm going to get you!" Then you can come out from either side of the baby for the "Gotcha!" grab. *Caution:* This variation is for babies who are familiar with their environment, and who already enjoy playing frontal Gotcha!

Suggestions: If the baby shows signs of unhappiness or fear, stop the game for an intermission of cuddling and soft talk. Continue the game later, if the baby is willing. Since the game has an element of surprise to it, a tired or hungry baby may not enjoy it. Initiate the baby when she is well rested and well fed.

12
Flyin' High

Purpose: To show the baby the amount of pleasure experienced from the unexpected or from a surprise
To help the baby enjoy games of suspense through the security of knowing that you are there to help

Equipment: None

Procedure:
1. Speaking in a quick, light tone to the baby, ask her if she wants to fly up in the air. Bounce the baby gently in your hands.
2. Swing the baby up just slightly higher than your head and release your grip from her sides just for a second. Say, "Wee!" Bring the baby down for a hug.
3. Repeat five to ten times if the baby continues to enjoy the game. Be sure to continue to laugh and show the baby that it's a game and that you are enjoying it. Stop occasionally to hug the baby.

43

Variation: Sing a lively tune or play a record that has a quick beat. Try "Pop! Goes the Weasel," for example. At the appropriate part or beat, toss the baby gently into the air.

Suggestion: If you are just starting this game, it's a good idea to be sure the baby is well fed and rested.

13
Story Time

Purpose: To acquaint the baby with the world of books and reading at a young age so she will always feel comfortable (as opposed to threatened) by them
To begin language development through repeated words and pictures
Calming activity for a game-playing baby whose bedtime is drawing near

Equipment: Clear, simple picture books, preferably with stiff cardboard pages. (Amy found that *Let's Eat*—aptly named!—was not only her favorite book to look at, but also quite chewable. She could "read," and relieve those nasty teething pains at the same time.)

Position: Sit with the baby in your lap, identify it by placing your hand on it saying, "Book. Let's read Amy's book."

Position: Sit with the baby in your lap, on the floor or in a chair. Hold the book in front of both you and the baby.

Procedure:

1. Before opening the book, identify it by placing your hand on it and saying, "Book. Let's read Amy's book."

2. Open the book to the first page and either read the text, or just point to different objects, calling them by name. "See the bear. See the bear's eyes." Your voice should be enthusiastic, but calm and quiet.

3. If the baby should inadvertently point to something on the page, be sure to call it by name—that is, stop and "discuss" the object.

14
What's the Diff?
(Part II)

Purpose: To give the baby an opportunity to experience how textures and forms change
To teach simple cause and effect
To introduce the sound of crumpling paper
Another game to calm baby after the suspense games or day's activities

Equipment: Old newspapers, magazines

Position: Put the baby on the floor, sit opposite her.

Procedure:
1. Crumple the paper. Say, "Listen!" Put the baby's hand on the jagged outer edge of the paper. Say, "Rough!"
2. Smooth out the paper. Put the baby's hand on it. Say, "Smooth."
3. Give the paper to the baby. Say, "Now, *you* do it."
4. Tear the paper—first one piece, then several. Listen to the sound together.

48

PART 4

Six to Nine
Months

Imitation Games

Once you've taught your baby a few imitation
games, you'll find they will save your life on long trips
when the baby is stuck in the car seat. Some games,
like good old Pat-a-cake, have a life expectancy of
several years. Once mastered, these games can be
useful for a long time with a little alteration.

Many casual actions, which adults take for
granted, can be challenging imitation games for
baby, adding creativity to her play periods. Julie and
Jerry taught Amy several games of this type that
gave Amy an opportunity to play independently,
and her parents a chance to get their work done.

Little Amy, the flirt, learned to tilt her head
sideways by imitating Julie and Jerry. We all thought
this was adorable; outsiders probably thought she
had something wrong with her neck! Another family
treat was the raspberry noise. Driving along, Jerry
would do it, then Julie, and after a pause, Amy. Then
everybody would laugh. Of course, you play this at

your own risk, because when the baby begins to do it on her own, it can be embarrassing!

More endearing were the little pats on the back one would receive when holding Amy. Waving bye-bye, although socially acceptable, is usually disappointing, as the hand action always seems to come *after* the person you're trying to impress has driven away. Best of all imitations, of course, is giving kisses. Nothing is sweeter than one of those moist touches on the cheek! Following are some of our favorite games of imitation.

15
Pat-a-cake

Purpose: To develop concentration by watching the model
To improve coordination by making hands meet in rhythm

Equipment: None

Position: Sit opposite each other.

Procedure:
1. Say, "Pat-a-cake, pat-a-cake, baker's man." (four hand claps)
"Bake me a cake as fast as you can." (four hand claps)
"Pat it" (pretend to be kneading)
"And prick it" (as with a fork)
"And mark it with ——" (baby's first initial)
"And put it in the oven" (pretend to do so)
"For baby and me!" (hug)
2. Take the baby's hands and say the rhyme again, guiding the baby's hands in the motions.
3. Say, "Amy, can *you* do Pat-a-cake?"

4. Repeat this procedure several times a day to help the baby remember.

Variations: This is fun in the bath (lots of splashing), and can save your sanity on a long car trip. You can always play Pat-a-cake with baby's feet. The soles make a snapping sound that babies love.

16
Backward Peek-a-boo

Purpose: Training in coordination at a higher
level than has been previously taught
To stimulate baby's thinking process by
applying a learned skill in a new way

Equipment: A bath towel or a dish towel

Position: Put the baby on her back on a towel
after her bath.

Procedure: 1. Start the game by whisking the top
edge of the baby's towel over her
face, saying, "Where's Amy?
Where's Amy?" Whisk it right away,
saying, "*There* she is!"
2. Lay the towel tip over the baby's
face, leave it there, and say,
"Where's Amy?" If the baby yanks
it off say, "*There* she is!" and laugh.
If the baby doesn't pull off the towel,
count to ten, later to twenty, before
pulling it off. Patience—the baby
will catch on!

Variations: The baby can cover her dog with a dish
towel. Or, you can sit beside the baby

and put a scarf on her head; then let her cover you. This game can be played with a doll, too, and creates a welcome diversion during the squirmy while-having-diapers-changed stage.

Suggestion: Don't cover all of the baby's face—that's a little too scary.

17
The Writing Bug

Purpose: To improve small-muscle coordination in the hands
To develop concentration—necessary to imitate this action

Equipment: Paper and toy drumstick or similar toy

Position: Seat the baby in her high chair or in a booster seat at the table where you are working. Place paper and "writing" tool in front of baby. Sit at your own work place near baby.

Procedure:
1. Explain to the baby that you are both doing the same thing: "Well, look at us—Mommy is correcting papers, and so is Amy!"
2. Help the baby to hold her writing tool, and guide her hand to make marks on the paper (just impressions).
3. Baby will stab wildly at pad of paper. Continue talking and encouraging her in her "work."

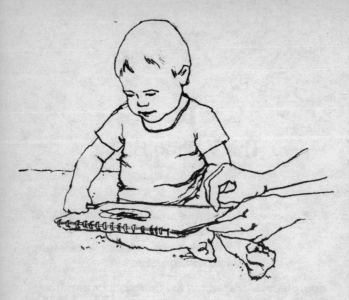

Variations: An old typewriter (garage-sale variety) set up beside yours lends an added dimension to the Writing Bug game.

Suggestion: Keep a back-up book, magazine, and cracker handy, as attention span is short on this one, especially at the beginning. However, this game can be prolonged for a surprising length of time if properly taught at the beginning—long enough to balance a checkbook, make out a market list, or write a letter.

18

Here, a Weed;
There, a Weed

Purpose: To develop small-muscle coordination in the hand
To improve baby's ability to imitate
To provide an opportunity for an outdoor activity, essential to healthy growth

Equipment: Small trowel and bucket

Position: Have baby sit, stand, squat, or even crawl near you as you weed.

Procedure:
1. Give the baby a demonstration on how to weed. Say, "Watch Daddy." Put your fingers around the weed and pull it up.
2. Say, "You try weeding now." Put your fingers around the baby's hand and guide it to a weed. Help her pull it up. Say, "Good girl, Amy! You got a big fat one!"
3. Continue your weeding, while the baby continues to pick at weeds. Stop from time to time to show her again, and to help her pull one. (Also, check to make sure it is *weeds*

she is working on, and not Daddy's long-awaited dichondra lawn!)

Variation: This game can easily be adapted to planting bulbs. You will need an extra trowel and bucket. Follow the same procedure as in Here a Weed, being sure to demonstrate and reinforce the skills being taught.

Suggestions: This is a dirty game, so be sure baby is wearing work clothes. On a warm day, a little water (making mud) can keep a baby quite busy long after you've done the weeding, and maybe some trimming, too!

19

Kitchen Patrol

Purpose: To develop skill in discriminating between shapes and sizes
To develop hand coordination
To encourage verbal development

Equipment: Any kitchen equipment similar to whatever the playing partner is using; for instance, measuring spoons and cups, a bowl and wooden spoon. You'll need a plastic bottle of cooking oil with a tight lid, too.

Position: Seat baby in a high chair or on the floor, but not underfoot.

Procedure:
1. As you begin your cooking, explain to the baby that you are both doing the same thing. Say, "Good girl, Amy! Help Mommy get dinner ready. We need a bowl, a spoon, and a measuring cup." Hand her the utensils as you name them.
2. Explain to the baby what you are doing, step by step. As you begin a step she can imitate, show her how you do it, and guide her hands in

imitation. "Okay, Amy, after we add the flour, we *stir.*" Show her and guide her hands. "Then we pour in the oil." Show and guide (of course, her oil doesn't come out— it's just pretend). Say, "Can you do that?" Always say, "Good girl!" (or boy).

3. Continue the game as long as necessary (after the sauce is simmering on the stove), repeating the same actions, so the baby will remember the game.

Suggestions:

1. Until the baby becomes proficient in stirring and pouring (all pretend), her attention may wander. A drawer at her level filled with safe kitchen utensils can keep a baby happy for quite some time. A pair of tongs was a favorite toy of Amy's, but when she learned to zap them onto the dog's tail he had to slink out of reach—no more spilled tidbits for him!

2. *Caution:* Don't attempt to teach this game when you're in a hurry. Like the Writing Bug, this game takes time and patience. It pays off, though, because sometime when you really *are* in a hurry, you won't have the baby hanging onto your leg, or demanding to sit in your lap at the desk.

20

The Human Schmoo, or Roly-poly

Purpose:	To develop spatial awareness To grasp the concepts of *up* and *down*
Equipment:	None
Position:	Sit on floor with baby beside you.
Procedure:	1. Fall flat on your back, and say, "Oh, oh! I fell *down!*"
	2. Put your arm out, helplessly, and say, "Can you help pull me *up?* Pull me *up!*"
	3. Touch baby. Spring right back up into a sitting position. Say, "*Thank* you. You got me up!"
	4. Baby usually reaches out for you again right away (and you can pretend to be pushed over); but if she doesn't, you fall down again, saying, "Oh, oh," etc.
	5. After several repetitions, when baby has the hang of pushing you over, don't flop down right away. When

she pushes you, say, "Oh, you'll have to push harder than that!" The baby will push. You waver a bit, but remain upright. Baby pushes; after two tries (on the third try) you fall over.

Variation: Block-building and knocking-down—especially knocking-down—is an activity based on this same aggressive behavior. Lots of fun, if you're in the mood.

21
Steamroller

Purpose: To further develop baby's large-muscle coordination
To develop baby's perception of herself in relation to the rug or mat

Equipment: None

Position: Put the baby on her back on the rug or a mat.

Procedure:
1. Get down on your hands and knees, and lower your head like a bull. Make sure the baby can see you coming!
2. Gently roll the baby from her back to her stomach, using your head. Make a noise like a rumbling engine. Say, "Now, I'm going to roll you over!" Keep talking and laughing.
3. Put the baby back on her back. Say, "Here I come again!" (Rumble, rumble.) Push the baby all the way over from her back to her stomach to her back again. Repeat this step.

Variation: You can also play this game by rolling the baby with your hands, pushing gently.

Suggestions: To avoid having the baby crawl away, go slowly; also, don't roll her too far. Instead, *you* crawl around to her other side and push her back using your head.

22
Grab It

Purpose: To teach timing and eye-hand coordination

Equipment: A bright-colored toy

Position: Sit opposite each other.

Procedure:
1. Sit in front of the baby. Hold out a familiar bright-colored toy, and say, "Here, Amy, do you want your—?" Reach your hand out, as if you're going to give it to her. Then, in a joking way, laugh and say, "Wait a minute. I want to look at it again." Pull the toy back to yourself.
2. Now begin to hand the toy to the baby again. As she reaches for it, pull it back, laughing.
3. Hold the toy out, and let the baby grab it. Say, "Oh! You got it!" (Big hug, laugh.)

Variations: If, when you reach out to take the toy back and thus start a new round of Grab It, the baby pulls the toy back, laugh. Then very slowly put your hand out; let

it barely touch the toy. If the baby doesn't pull back, take the toy. If she does pull back, let her trick you twice before taking the toy. Say, "Let me have the toy!" Laugh!

Suggestions: This game has a teasing quality, a surprise element, that makes it fun—the baby expects the toy to be in her hand, and it's not. But you must always give the baby the toy the third time, that's the rule! It's not meant to be a mean game, so don't continue if the baby doesn't think it's funny. Play Grab It at diaper-changing or getting-dressed time with three people—you, the baby, and the person who's changing or dressing the squirmy infant. *Caution:* Play this game for short periods only.

23
Tub Time

Purpose: To help baby adjust to a full-size tub, if
she hasn't done so already
To help baby enjoy the bath and to
avoid a fear of water

Equipment: In addition to your usual bath necessities, you'll need a nonbreakable cup
and an assortment of about five bath
toys—plastic boat, fish, Ping-Pong ball,
spongy starfish, whale

Position: Baby sits in well-filled tub with partner
on stool beside the tub.

Procedure: 1. Name each item as you give it to the
baby, and show her what it does.
2. When the toys are all assembled in
the bath, allow a few minutes for the
baby to play with them.
3. As you begin to wash the baby's
hair, give her a toy to wash, too.
After using the shampoo bottle,
hand it to the baby and encourage
her to put shampoo on her toys.
Say, "Now, you wash the fish's hair.

Pour the shampoo out and rub it in." Help her, so she uses just a little. As you rinse the baby's hair, follow the same procedure. Say, "Pour the water (use the plastic cup) over the fish's head to rinse out the shampoo. Careful! Don't get it in his eyes!"

4. Continue this activity as the soap and washcloth are used.

5. After the baby is all washed, let her play a few minutes more with her various toys.

Variation: Peek-a-boo behind the shower door or curtain is a nice, quiet game to play after a rowdy bath, or to cheer up a baby who's gotten soap in her eyes.

Suggestions: A baby who dislikes water on her face could be encouraged to splash about, getting used to the water before actually being washed. Amy loved to splash— and rarely needed rinsing!

24
Animal Introductions

Purpose: To familiarize baby with different animals—their actions and sounds
To find something to do with stuffed animals other than decorate a bed

Equipment: An assortment of stuffed animals in a basket or box

Position: Place the baby in a sitting position on the floor. Sit in front of the baby with the stuffed animals in the basket beside her.

Procedure:
1. As each stuffed animal is lifted from the basket, explain the following about it: its name, what sound it makes, how it walks or flies, and any other information you care to volunteer. Then move the animal next to the baby, and encourage her to hold it and to imitate its sound. Continue this procedure until all the stuffed animals are out of the basket.
2. Push the basket close to the baby, and encourage her to put the ani-

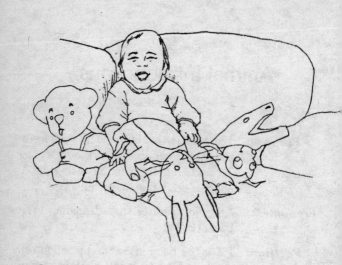

mals *back*. Say the name or make the sound as each animal returns to the basket. This reinforces the new learning *and* keeps the toys picked up!

Variation: Making the animals talk to the baby can really captivate her attention. Amy's favorite stuffed toy was a large bee that said, "I am a bee; I say buzzzz. Be careful of me or I might sting you!" She would laugh out loud as the bee zeroed in for the sting.

Suggestion: A group of dolls or plastic animals, or even assorted toys, can be adopted to this game as a way of introducing things the baby doesn't yet know what to do with.

25
Sing-a-long

Purpose: To encourage a sense of rhythm
To provide a basis for verbal imitation and expression

Equipment: None

Procedure:
1. Choose a song that has a repeating chorus or series of lines. A good song to start with is "Old Mac-Donald Had a Farm."
2. Sing the song through once, using as many hand and facial expressions as possible.
3. Sing the song again, and after the chorus, say to the baby, "Now, you sing, "E-i-e-i-o!" Reward any kind of a response with, "Good girl!"

Variation: More than one person singing seems to have an almost hypnotic effect on babies, so if you want peace in the car, don't be embarrassed—Sing-a-long!

Suggestion: Before going on a long car trip, you might pick up a simple song book—they're a real gold mine.

26
Puppet Play

Purpose: To help develop small- and large-muscle coordination in the hands
To encourage independent play through imitation

Equipment: Any variety of puppets—stuffed animal puppets, paper bag puppets, finger puppets

Procedure:
1. Placing puppet on hand or finger, begin by introducing it to the baby. "Hi, I'm Wally Walrus!" Continue by getting the baby involved. Say, "You must be Amy! Can you give me a kiss?" Or, "I'm going to tickle your tummy!"
2. Continue the conversation between the puppet and the baby. It could include Peek-a-boo, naming parts of the puppet ("Where are my eyes?"), singing, Pat-a-cake, or dancing.
3. Ask the baby if she wants to make the puppet dance, or whatever. She

may be reluctant to put a puppet over her whole hand; if so, see if she's willing to try one on her finger. Then ask her to make the puppet talk. Acknowledge any response with a hug.

Variations: Using both hands, two puppets can talk back and forth, including the baby in their "conversation." Finger-puppet people can be stuck on all five fingers and really have a great time!

PART 5

Nine Months to One Year

Roughhousing

This is an active period. Babies crawl around, exploring the house, play hockey by pushing a ball along in front of them with a stick or rattle or wooden spoon (to bang it with), just like a kitten. When the baby begins to walk holding on to furniture, a new realm of games opens up. Amy became very proficient at scooting along the edges of furniture and flinging herself at anyone sitting in close proximity, attempting to initiate a game of Gotcha! Or, leaning against the coffee table, Amy and her Daddy would roll a ball back and forth; outside, they would play Catch until Daddy got tired of trying to protect the creeping fig from Amy's wild shots!

27
Grandma's Game

Purpose: To develop large-muscle coordination
To develop eye-hand coordination

Equipment: None

Procedure:
1. Take baby for a walk. Look for a house with shallow, far-apart steps, where no one seems to be home (carport empty, curtains drawn, etc.). Holding the baby's hand, walk up the steps, turn around and walk down again. After a few trips, encourage the baby to go alone, catching her as she jumps off the bottom step, saying, "Good girl!" Plan to spend about ten minutes on the sidewalk. At the top step, Amy usually turned and made a short oration; this was her own variation.
2. Look for large metal plates in the sidewalk—it's hollow underneath. Stamp on this plate a few times, encouraging the baby to stamp, too. At the next one, she'll stamp, and you can say, "Good girl!"

3. Look for a fence with a knothole in it. This is good for poking shrubbery buds through.

4. Look for a little water running in the gutter. This is good for floating bits of leaves in.

Variations: Listen for a lawnmower—they are fun to watch. Also, big kids skate-boarding or shooting baskets are entertaining to observe.

Suggestions: A good walk lasts about twenty minutes. Establish a pattern with the same three or four activities done every time.

28
Yank

Purpose: This game affords lots or practice in crawling—really speeds it up!

Equipment: None

Position: Two adults plus baby are required. Baby and you on floor in crawling position; second adult five feet away

Procedure:
1. First adult calls to the baby to come across the room: "Come on, Amy, come to Grandma!" The baby will, naturally, start to crawl to those outstretched arms.
2. When the baby gets just within arm's reach, the other player quickly crawls after her, and gently pulls her back (by the seat of her sleepers or creepers) to the starting place. Hug baby. Say, "Oh, no you don't!"
3. The first player now calls enticingly again. Let the baby crawl longer this time (Grandma, move back!), and possibly she will flop down and wait

to be Yanked. Sometimes it takes two or three attempts to escape before the baby catches on to the game. When she flops, wait a few seconds (suspense!), then pull her back. Say, "You didn't think I was going to get you, did you?" Hug. Repeat five to ten times.

Variations: Have the baby crawl longer distances; have the player to whom the baby is crawling "rescue" her (scoop her up), just as she is about to be Yanked.

Suggestions: Not for the tired or hungry! Play on rug or suitable safe surface.

29
Gotcha! (Part II)

Purpose: Gotcha! II requires a higher level of thinking skills—the baby must select the appropriate time (and person) to play the game with her. This is the first time the baby is taught a game which she can initiate independently, at least where another player is involved. Timing is important here; and perception, too. The baby must do the "zeroing in."

Equipment: None

Position: Three players are required. You are lying on a couch or sitting in a low chair. The baby is playing on the rug nearby. Someone else is in the room.

Procedure:
1. Call to the baby. Say, "Come on and get me!" As the baby approaches, draw her near to you and, pretending fright, say, "Aghh! You got me!"
2. Put the baby back down and say, "Go get ——!" (Grandma or Daddy, etc.). Give the baby a little push

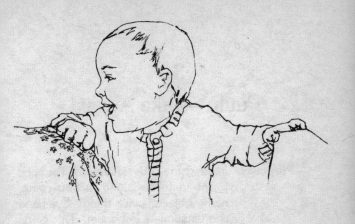

toward the "unsuspecting" intended victim. As she gets close, the second victim can copy the first—draw the baby to him, act scared, and say, "You got me!"

3. Second "Gotchee" sends baby back to first "Gotchee," saying in a whisper, "Go get ——." Got it?

Note: A baby who is a good Gotcha! player tends to attack unsuspecting guests—but you have to be pretty hardhearted not to be flattered when a baby hurls herself into your arms!

30
Put in—Take Away

Purpose: In this game, order is stressed. The baby learns to follow along as you count, name objects, place things. Eye-hand coordination is important. This game has a soothing, quieting effect on its players.

Equipment: About ten small toys or a book with heavy cardboard pages picturing simple toys

Position: You and baby side by side on a sofa with a basket of toys or a picture book of toys.

Procedure:
1. In a sort of rhythmical voice say, "Here's your turtle." Hand the baby her toy turtle.
2. Say, "May I have the turtle?" Put your hand out. The baby will give it to you. If not, gently take it away.
3. Say, "Here's your turtle." Hand it to the baby. Ask, "May I have the turtle?"
4. Say, "Here's your turtle." Hand it to baby. Say, "And here's your duck."

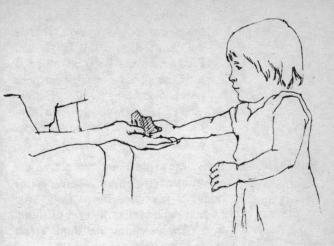

Hand it to baby. Say, "And here's your frog." Hand it to baby. Now these toys are either floating in the tub, or piled beside the baby.

5. Ask, "May I have the turtle?" Hold out your hand. Name whatever you get. "Oh, that's your duck!" When you have all the toys in your lap, hand them, one by one, back to the baby, counting or naming them as you do.

Variations: 1. The baby will soon initiate this game, handing you things one at a time for you to name. You should set them in a row beside you so that the baby can take them back without help. This way, the baby learns to play the game alone, a great help on long trips, or when you're too busy to play with her.

2. Sit by the baby and turn the pages of the picture book, saying, "There's the duck; there's the frog"; etc. Pretty soon the baby will want to turn the pages herself. (Put your hand over hers; say, "Gently, gently.") A baby will sit with a book for quite a while, turning the pages and murmuring to herself!

Suggestions: Babies like to put *in* and take *out*, as well as arrange items on a level area. A doll house is good for this activity or a kitchen cupboard or a bowl of round fruit. (Always check that items aren't going in the baby's mouth.)

31
Play Ball!

Purpose: To develop large-muscle coordination
To develop hand-eye perception

Equipment: Any bright-colored, lightweight ball, about seven inches in diameter

Position: Sit opposite the baby—about five feet away.

Procedure: 1. Roll the ball to the baby. Hold out your hands, saying, "Roll the ball back to me!"

2. The baby will fling it back toward you. If she doesn't, take the ball away, and try again until she does.

3. After a few rolls to the baby, and baby's return rolls to you—straight up or behind her; baby returns are unpredictable!—try a soft bounce to her. Pretty soon the baby will be bouncing the ball back to you; and that's how you Play Ball!

Variation: This is fun to play on the beach.

Suggestion: If the baby doesn't want to fling the ball back to you, she's not ready for this game, so drop it.

32

Dance with Me
(Part II)

Purpose: To encourage the baby's sense of rhythm
To help the baby hear the beat

Equipment: A music box or a record player and records

Position: Baby must be able to stand unaided.

Procedure: If you have been dancing with your baby all along, this game-activity will be easy to teach.

1. Put on the record. Hold the baby's hands in yours, and "dance" from side to side, swaying your body, but not moving your feet.

2. Say to the baby, "Let's dance!" You "dance," but don't hold the baby's hands. She will imitate you. If she doesn't, hold one hand for a while longer.

3. Let go of the baby's hand and let her try again. The baby soon will enjoy "dancing" by herself.

Suggestion: The baby's attention span is short, so don't expect her to dance to much more than the first two or three bars of music. Typically, then, babies will go on to other activities, stopping to dance from time to time as they renotice the music.

33

Ring Around the Rosy

Purpose: To develop a sense of rhythm and timing
To learn to dance in a circle

Equipment: None

Position: The baby has to be able to stand. You alone, or you and one or two other players, join hands, holding baby firmly.

Procedure:
1. Walking on tiptoe, in a clockwise circle, all sing, "Ring Around the Rosy. Pocketful of posies. Ashes, ashes, all fall down."
2. Emphasize the word *down*. Dramatically sit, then immediately fall backward. As you sit, gently *let* the baby down; don't pull her. Roll back, so your feet fly up in the air. (You've really got to clown it up for this one.)
3. Spring back up into a sitting position. Then stand up; baby up, too. Repeat song and dance. Amy couldn't seem to make it all the way

to "all fall down" at first—she tried to flop down at "Pocketful of posies," and had to be dragged along to the bitter end.

Suggestions: This game increases in value the more you play it because soon she can play it with others (siblings and cousins who love it), and it's great at Thanksgiving and other family gatherings.

34
Hockey, Anyone?

Purpose: To develop hand-eye coordination
To develop concepts such as *under,
behind, in front of,* etc.

Equipment: A wooden spoon or small, flat stick like a
tongue depressor. You will also need a
small ball (a Ping-Pong ball is just right).

Position: Place the baby in a crawling position on
the floor with the ball out in front of her.
Sit or kneel beside her.

Procedure:
1. Give the ball a gentle tap with the
stick or spoon, saying, "Hey! There
goes the ball! Daddy hit the ball with
the spoon!" Give the ball another
tap, sending it back toward the
baby, saying, "Look, Daddy hit it
again!"
2. Say, "Now, *you* try, Amy. Hit the
ball!" Hand her the stick, and guide
her hand in a swinging motion so
she taps the ball.
3. Encourage the baby to crawl after
the ball (give her a little push), and

hit it again. If she is reluctant, hit it
back to her, and repeat step 2.

4. After several demonstrations, the
baby will probably be crawling
around happily, swiping away at the
ball until it becomes wedged under
a chair or behind a couch. At this
point, the partner will have to fish it
out in order to keep the game going.

Variations: Hockey, Anyone? is as much fun, if not
more, when the partner continues to
play with the baby, batting the ball to
the baby and letting the baby bat it back
to him.

Suggestions: This is an easy game to take visiting; put
the equipment in your purse, and the
baby can play while you catch up on the
news.

35
Story Time (Part II)

Purpose: To continue developing language skills through repeated words and pictures
To encourage the baby to enjoy her books
To improve small-muscle coordination

Equipment: Simple picture books. At this time also add nursery rhyme books and some Dr. Seuss.

Position: Sit with the baby on the floor or in a chair, holding the book out in front of both of you.

Procedure:
1. If the baby is familiar with books, and has been playing Story Time all along, begin by asking her if she wants to read a book. "Amy, do you want to read a book? Is it story time?" The older baby (twelve months) may even bring a book to you after this query.
2. Hold the book by its cover and leave the pages free for the baby to turn. If she has difficulty, help her. As she turns the pages, name the objects

on the page or read the rhyme.
Sometimes this may be difficult.
Amy became more intrigued with
seeing how fast she could turn the
pages than with reading or looking
at the book. We came up with some
fairly garbled nursery rhymes,
reading only the first line from each
one!

3. Continue to identify the same object
again and again. Soon the baby will

be able to point it out to you when asked "Where's the eye?" for example. Imitate animal sounds as you come to their pictures. Ask the baby, "Can you do that? What does the cow say?"

Suggestions: 1. There are books on the market that use life-size photographs of shoes, hairbrushes, apples, etc. These make excellent games because you can show the baby the real red tennis shoe on her foot and then the picture of the shoe. The baby might try to brush her hair with the pictured hairbrush or put the book's tennis shoe on her foot—they are so real!

2. Take a favorite book, or a new one, to the restaurant when you take the baby. Either before dinner arrives and after the crackers are all gone, or after the baby is through eating but you're not, there's nothing like a good book to save the day.

36
Jerry's Hide-and-Chase Game

Purpose: To teach a baby how to anticipate re-
sults
To enjoy a sequence of actions
To develop walking and running skills
To increase attention span

Equipment: None

Position: Three players are required. The first
player kneels on the floor, holding the
standing baby against his knees. The
other player stands about ten feet away,
facing the baby.

Procedure: 1. Warm-up activity: The player holding the baby says, "Go get Daddy!"
(Give the baby a little push.) The
other player takes a few steps away
from the baby, pretending to be
scared. Say, "Amy's going to get
me!" He lets himself be caught.

2. Warm-up activity: The caught
player kneels, and sends the baby
back to the other player, saying,
"Go get Mommy!" This player gets
up, pretends to be scared, goes a

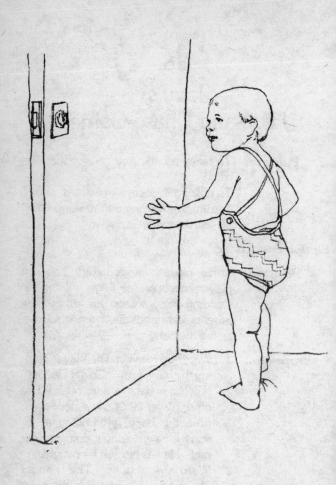

little farther, but gets caught, hugs baby.

3. First player repeats steps 1 and 2. Then, the person pretending to run will start to run, and then turn around and run *at* the baby, saying, "Why am I running away from you? You're littler than I am!"

4. The other player calls out, "Run, run—run back to Mommy!" The baby will turn, run, and hurl herself into the waiting player's arms (they love that) in glee at having escaped this fate worse than death. Repeat this step until the baby has learned all the tricks of the game thus far—it may take three or four weeks.

5. One player runs and hides around the corner in an adjoining room. Then the other player says, "Go find Daddy!" Head the baby off in the right direction. When the baby finds the player, that person jumps out and howls at her like a monster! The other player calls, "Come, come! Run, run!" and the baby will run full force down the hall (with the monster thudding at her heels) and fling herself into safety's waiting arms.

6. Finally, one player can go and hide, and you can say to the baby, "Go find Daddy!" and Jerry's Hide-and-Chase Game is off and running!

Suggestions: Be sure to change roles often—the same person shouldn't always be the "monster." Also, check that nothing is blocking the baby's path when chasing, or you'll have tears instead of squeals of joy.

37

Grandfather's Game

Purpose: To develop whole-body balance, timing, large-muscle coordination

Equipment: Any kind of stairs, outside or in

Position: Hold the baby's hands with a finger from each of your hands. Stand behind her at the top of a short flight of steps.

Procedure:
1. Walking with the baby in front of you, go down one step. Say, "Good girl, you made it!" Turn the baby around, still holding her hands, and go *up* the one step. Say, "Good girl, you made it!"
2. Try the same procedure on four or five steps, staying with her both up and down.
3. Hold only one hand; same procedure, same encouraging words.
4. Let the baby go it alone, but stay behind her.
5. After a few weeks, the baby will be able to go up and down a flight of ten steps without help, as long as

you are nearby to catch her triumphant glances at both bottom and top of the flight, and say, "Good girl, you made it!"

Variations: Babies love the challenge of steps. On a walk around the block, keep your eye out for a likely twosome or foursome of steps where you can sit down while baby plays.

Suggestion: Always remain nearby; visiting, but watching.

Conclusion

If you have ever held a baby and had her start to cry—if you have known that awful panic—this little book of games might help you to cope more successfully the next time an infant crosses your path. Playing with a baby involves serious effort, and we hope that grandparents, parents, siblings, and baby-sitters will learn the rules, and practice our games with a handy baby. You don't have to stick exactly to our schedule, but do try to start with the early games, so that the baby will have the skills necessary to enjoy the later ones. We think your baby will learn a lot about creative playing, as well as how to entertain herself. And we hope you will discover and enjoy the variety of activities that it is possible to share with someone who cannot talk, walk, or even, in the beginning, sit up without help. Don't forget to laugh and to hug. Have a good time!

Book II

MORE
GAMES
BABIES
PLAY

*Fun with Babies from Birth
Through the First Birthday*

For my husband Jerry,
a loving father.
And to Amy and Katie,
the joys of our life.

Contents

PART FIVE:
NINE TO TWELVE MONTHS
Action Games

Preface

This is a book filled with games. There are games for tiny infants, stimulating action or soothing play. There are games for crawlers, climbers, or prewalkers. For the feeling-left-out older brother or sister there are games they can play, too. These are games we played with our two children, Amy and Kate (which is why we will always refer to "she"—just set in our ways), and we want to share them with anyone who wants to enjoy their small children now while they still let you play with them!

When you first had your baby, do you remember all those grandmothers, aunts, and neighbor ladies who said, "Oh! Enjoy her now. They grow up so fast! She'll be starting school before you know it!"? I do. I thought they were crazy. "Starting school," I remember thinking, "she isn't even starting solids yet!" But, you know what? They were right! Children do grow up fast, and if you're not careful, you can miss it. In those first few years you are the main source of information and entertainment. Even if you're a working parent, you can be the most powerful influence on your child because it is the quality of the time spent with her, not the quantity, that really counts. You are the center of the universe; you know everything and can do anything, as far as your baby or toddler is concerned. Take advantage of this because the day will come, sooner than you think, when the front door will be thrown open and a small familiar voice will call, "We're all going to Leah's and I need to take Vickie (the doll). Bye!" The door will bang shut and you'll have a very funny feeling inside you. Proud, I think I felt, but also, yes, I admit, a bit left out. And I remember thinking, "My gosh, they grow up fast!"

So here is a book to help you get started, because you'll find that every time you play a game, you'll think up something different to do, until you've made up a new game! Relax and have fun and then you won't feel so bad when your three year old calls you on the phone to ask if she can go to the movies with the neighbors!

And then there's another side to game-playing. It can save your life and your sanity. Some days there's a crisis every time you turn around: from putting on shoes and getting in (or out of) the car to washing the hair and going to bed. And as you come up against each hurdle you find yourself rapidly falling apart. As most books will tell you, distraction is often the best way to leap these hurdles. And if you have a quick game on the tip of your tongue, you'll get those fingernails clipped a lot faster than you could using physical force, and you won't be nearly as exhausted either!

A game as a reward for a job well done is also a good motivator. After all, it's better for her than candy, has immediate effect, and is less expensive than toys—only costing you a few moments of your time. What a bargain! So read on and spend freely—it's worth every second!

Acknowledgments

A special thank you is in order for my most supportive helper, typist, and, above all, baby-sitter—a best friend, my mother. This book wouldn't have been possible without her.

And, once again, thanks to my good friend Ann Shaw (and little Rebecca) for posing in photo sessions.

Introduction

Just as our first book, *Games Babies Play,* was inspired by our experiences with our first daughter, Amy, *More Games Babies Play* is thanks to her sister, Kate. But the games in this book, while they can easily be played by an adult alone with a baby, are also designed to include an older child or children.

When I came home from the hospital, I was more worried about three-year-old Amy than I was about three-day-old Kate. My love and concern for my first child was so overwhelming that I felt guilty. But as Amy tried my patience again and again in the next few weeks, those feelings of love were often replaced by frustration, disappointment, and, yes, anger.

I know I am not the only mother who was just seated to feed her baby when her older child absolutely *had* to have a glass of juice. Poor Kate made many a speed run to the refrigerator, still clinging to the bottle or breast (which is a good trick!). Amy discovered all kinds of interesting facts in those first weeks. She found that a harmonica sounds loudest next to a sleeping baby's door and she decided that baby formula actually tasted quite awful, although she didn't want to admit it. She learned that Mom could move a lot quicker than you'd expect when baton twirling was practiced above Kate's head, and that you can get a whole roomful of company to gasp all at once just by touching the top of a baby's head! But most interesting of all were the things Amy learned about babies themselves. Much to my distress Amy found out that when you try to pick up a baby by yourself, the head flops back, and that babies really don't like the washcloth wrung out over their faces. She also learned that babies cry when you pull the bottle out of their mouths, pull their hair (if they're lucky enough to have any), or squeeze their hands really tight. But, to a three year old, the most important and yet frustrating fact about babies is that they don't seem to be good for anything. They can't talk, walk, or play games. Or can they?

As the three of us were squished into the rocking chair one morning, Kate over my shoulder, Amy on my lap rubbing Kate's back to help burp her, we played our first game together. Taking turns, we sang a spontaneous song. The words we made up were, "One, two, three girls in a rocking chair, early in the morning." The song began to grow as we kept the same tune but made up new lyrics about the three of us in the rocking chair. We sang about colors we saw, food we liked, and people we knew. We sang about silly, pretend things, "I have a cow living in my closet," and real things, "Did you know bears sleep all the winter through?" Keeping the same tune, we sang our song over and over again. Then suddenly it dawned on me—I was enjoying my children. Kate had fallen peacefully asleep snuggled against my neck. It wasn't the first time she'd been rocked to sleep, but I'm sorry to say that at three weeks it was probably the first time she'd been sung to sleep. Amy was relaxed and happy and I felt all those feelings of love rushing back; a first for both of us in those busy weeks, too.

So we continued to play games together. Of course our problems were not over. Squeeze the Head, firmly discouraged by the rest of us, remained one of Amy's favorites for a long time! But we had discovered a way to play games with Kate that included Amy so that we could all feel good about Kate being a baby, Amy being a big sister, and Mom not having to say, "No, leave her alone!" so much anymore. I taught Amy, so she could teach them to Kate, the games I had played with her when she was a baby, and then we made up the new ones you'll find here. And the more we played, and the more Kate grew, the more fun we had.

So, for the mother who hears herself say, "No, honey, she really doesn't like to be pulled across the room by her legs," or for the friend who says, "I think that's enough pushes on the baby swing" as the baby practically flies out of her seat, or for the daddy in the park who calls, "You better let me push the stroller now. You're going too fast near those trees!" this book of games might help you channel that young energy into play while also giving you a chance to get to know your new baby. And for those of you who are lucky enough to be first-time parents, grandparents, aunts, or uncles, we hope you will find these games stimulating and real lifesavers while you learn to enjoy your baby!

—J. H.

PART 1
Birth to Six Weeks

Awareness Games

The world must seem overwhelming to a new baby—all those sights, sounds, smells, and feelings coming from everywhere. It's your job to help your baby feel comfortable and secure in this big, sometimes scary, place, and a good way to introduce her* to it all is slowly and quietly. Most babies are frightened by quick, jerky movements or sharp, sudden sounds. Many of the games in this section include singing or talking to your baby. I know, it's pretty one-sided, but don't feel foolish—it's not as silly as talking to your plants! When singing or talking, do so in slow motion, letting your baby linger over each word. They love to watch your mouth move, too, so exaggerate! Remember to keep continual eye contact when possible.

These first weeks are crucial and even though "babies sleep all the time" (everyone says that but

---

*No offense, please, players with boy-baby partners, but we're going to stick to "her" throughout this book.

usually not the mother!), use those waking moments wisely!

If you have an older brother or sister at home and want him or her to participate, great!, but by all means play along with them, supervising carefully. You never know when a quick tug or rough roll might hurt or scare your baby.

We also found with Amy that she enjoyed Row, Row . . . and Now Hear This as much as Kate did. By all means play these games with your older kids. They'll feel good about the attention they're getting and, luckily, they get bored with them quickly, so just maybe you can lie down for a minute!

1
Row, Row,
Row Your Legs

Purpose: To relax tense muscles

Equipment: None

Position: Lay the baby on her back on a quilt. Sit or kneel beside her.

Procedure:
1. Hold the baby's feet gently and, *one leg at a time,* push the bent knee up to the chest.
3. Alternate legs, softly singing, "Row, row, row your legs gently up to tummy!"
3. When bringing the leg down be sure not to pull on the leg or force it if the baby is tense.
4. After several rounds of "Row, Row, Row . . ." the feet and legs can be massaged to further relax a tight baby.

Variation: For a baby enjoying herself, a few quick kisses on the bottom of the foot can be fun.

Suggestions: This game is best played without diapers, lending itself to before or after the

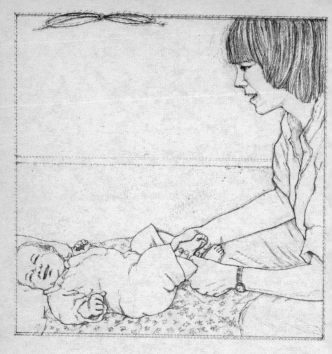

bath. Don't play for more than ten minutes at a time. This game never seems to lose its appeal. The older the baby becomes, the more she will enjoy it and the quicker your movements can be.

Including More Players: If including a small child in Row, Row, Row . . . let her sit in front of you and hold her arms as she pushes the baby's legs up and down. Teach her the words as you go and how to smile at the baby while singing. It's probably not a good idea to let a very young child (under four) play with a baby ten weeks or younger without an adult also playing. Amy got a charge out of "winding" Kate up, and after tiring of the game wanted her mommy to wind her up (as if she needed it, right?). I used to run pretend races, first "rowing" Kate gently, then Amy quickly to overtake Kate at the finish line!

2
Now Hear This!

Purpose: To stimulate the baby's sense of hearing
To introduce the baby to new sounds in everyday world

Equipment: None

Position: Lay the baby on her back on a quilt. Straddle your arms over baby, leaning over her face.

Procedure:

1. Begin by leaning your face close to the baby's. Call her name softly as she tries to focus in on your voice, say, "Kate, Kate, here's Mommy."
2. As baby "zeroes" in on your face, begin making a variety of sounds, not too loudly. Smacking the lips, clucking, whistling, all will attract the baby's attention.
3. Do just one sound at a time, following it with a smile and a "How did you like that one?" so she knows that you're still there.

Suggestions: A baby upset at a diaper change or waiting for a bottle will quiet

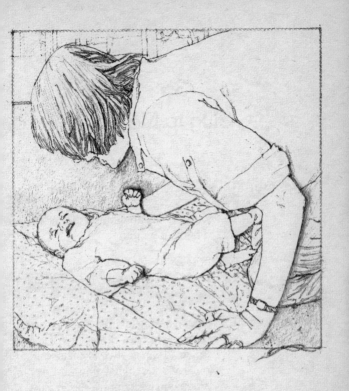

momentarily for a squeaking kiss noise as she tries to locate its source! Limit play time to about ten minutes with only, perhaps, five different sounds at a game.

Including More Players: This game adapts beautifully when including an older child. Kids can come up with some pretty fascinating sounds, sometimes gross, but always intriguing to a three week old!

3
Sing to Me

Purpose: To strengthen the baby's sense of rhythm
To widen her vocabulary by the repetition of familiar words

Equipment: Record player (optional)

Position: Stand or sit, holding the baby against your shoulder.

Procedure:
1. Think of a song (simple one!) whose words you know—at least two lines. We like "Twinkle, twinkle, little star! How I wonder what you are!" or "When you wish upon a star, makes no difference who you are."
2. Sway back and forth, singing and repeating your chosen song.
3. Now, keeping the same tune, *personalize* the song by changing the words and/or including the baby's name. Slip in the names of brothers and sisters—pets, too! After seeing the musical *Evita,* we sang, "Don't cry for me, Katie Hagstrom! You know I've never left you!"

138

4. Repeat the song four or five times before going on with another one.

Variation: Nursery rhymes can be sing-songed. "Amy and Katie, they lost their mittens. . . ."

Including More Players: If you have a chair big enough for three, you can sing, "One, two, three girls in a rocking chair. . . ." An older brother or sister might enjoy thinking up new words, also.

4

Eye to Eye

Purpose: To establish communication through eye contact

To make feeding a relaxed, pleasurable experience for mother and baby

Equipment: None

Position: Hold the baby in position to be fed.

Procedure:

1. After your baby is settled into her feeding, begin by gently stroking her cheek or face (if you have a free hand!) and softly saying her name.

2. When she is looking at you, smile, saying, "Hi, Kate! Look who I see, Kate!" Look directly at her, making clear eye contact as you speak.

3. Move your head very slowly from side to side while maintaining eye contact with your baby. Try to hold her attention with your eyes as well as your voice.

Suggestions: Often, a very young baby will not nurse (or drink a bottle) and open her eyes at the same time. She may want to shut

140

out extra stimulation in order to concentrate on eating—her biggest pleasure! You can't expect her to do two things at the same time so you can always play Eye to Eye just after feeding or while waiting for a burp!

If you have a big brother or sister at home, feeding the baby can get to be a hassle instead of a pleasure because of the many interruptions. Before settling down with the baby, set up your older child with a doll and a bottle. Boys can feed their Spider Man dolls, and even Darth Vader needs a bottle now and then!

You can continue the activity with diaper changing—side by side. And even a child's doll stroller is a good investment for walking your "babies" together. All of this proved to be a welcome reversal of roles for Amy; instead of pretending to be a baby, she could play the mommy for a change.

PART 2
Six to Twelve Weeks

Looking and Listening Games

The sixth week seems to be a turning point in babyhood. A pattern of sleeping and eating often develops, and outings on nice days can be stretched beyond going to the mailbox and back! A Snugglie front-pouch carrier is great for walks to the park or quick trips to the market because it leaves your hands free for pushing a swing, a shopping cart, or holding a small hand to cross the street.

At this age your baby may begin to recognize your face or voice. Kate loved anything with a face, or a reasonable facsimile, on it, and especially enjoyed a trip to the bathroom mirror. Your baby is beginning to look beyond herself to the world around her, so in this section of games there are games to introduce her to various sounds and sights which will stimulate her curiosity and encourage her to explore her surroundings.

5
Rhythm Band

Purpose: To broaden awareness of musical
sounds
To stimulate sense of rhythm

Equipment: Harmonica, wooden spoons, xylo-
phone, tambourine, kazoo, any musical
instruments or substitutes

Position: Place the baby in her infant seat while
you and any other players sit in front of
her.

Procedure: 1. Using any simple song you are
familiar with, sing while gently
playing (tapping, strumming) one of
your instruments.
2. Change to a different instrument but
continue with the same song to be
consistent in the rhythm.

Variation: Nursery rhymes work very well in tapping or jingling out a beat. This way you
can play in front of visitors and not be
embarrassed by your singing.

Suggestions: Be sure to play softly. If the baby startles
with an instrument, save it for another

time. Only play about three different instruments at each game session, letting her familiarize herself with them before introducing new ones. This game has real longevity depending on the number of "instruments" you can come up with!

Including More Players: A three or four year old can really have fun with this one. Amy often danced feverishly to my "tunes" while Katie watched, fascinated by the movement.

6
Snap 'n' Clap

Purpose: To distract an upset baby
To develop infant's eyesight coordination

Equipment: None

Position: Place the baby on her stomach on a quilt on the floor, or on her back in her infant seat.

Procedure:
1. Sit in front of the baby. Snap your fingers right in front of her face, so she can't miss it—three or four inches from her eyes.
2. Now, clap your hands sharply.
3. Repeat snap of fingers. Follow quickly by clap.
4. After a few snaps and claps, begin to chant, "Snap and clap, snap and clap! Watch Mommy snap and clap!" (Katie perks right up at this routine. It makes her forget whatever it was that was bothering her.)
5. Move your hands off to one side— not too far—she will follow the

147

movement with her eyes. Chant, "Over here, over here! Snap and clap off to the side." Try the other side for a quick windup.

Suggestion: This game is designed for quick relief—don't expect it to hold the baby's attention for very long.

Including More Players: Try not to laugh when the three year old struggles with finger snapping; they can clap just fine, and that's the main thing!

7
New Views

Purpose: To broaden baby's horizons and extend her waking time
To keep her interest in the outside world

Equipment: Infant seat

Procedure:
1. Strap the baby into her infant seat, and select a safe place to put her—somewhere new, like beside the sliding glass door so she can see the trees blowing outside.
2. After five minutes, move her to the floor beside the dishwasher. "Clank! Clank!" What can that intriguing noise be?
3. Put her on the dining room table, under the chandelier. Now, gently set it to swinging—that's good for ten minutes.

Variations: Next time, put her by the ticking clock or the radio.

Suggestion: Be sure you are nearby, wherever you move her. This is a good game if you're folding laundry or putting away the groceries. It's really an independent activity; more structured than just leaving her laying in her crib.

150

8
Driver Training

Purpose: To help develop eye-hand coordination, using small gestures

Position: Put the baby in her infant seat, facing you. Kneel in front of her.

Procedure:
1. Hold your hand out like a steering wheel, with all five fingers spread wide. Be sure the palm of your hand is in front of the baby's face.
2. Wriggle your fingers wildly to attract her attention.
3. Now, slip your thumb into the baby's right fist—ease it in, until she's got a good grip.
4. Tuck your little finger into the baby's other hand. Baby is now holding on to the "steering wheel" with both hands. All set?
5. Say, "Katie's going to Dr. Bray! Vroom! Vroom! Here we go!"
6. Gently move your hand in an arc from right to left, like a steering wheel—not too fast, or she'll lose her grip on your thumb and finger.

151

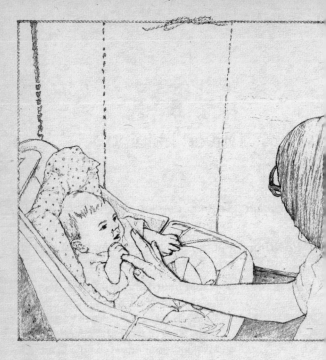

Suggestion: Babies love this game, so play away until your wrist tires.

Including More Players: When the older child sits in her car seat, steering her little wheel, you can give your hand to the baby so she can help drive; the older one can honk the horn and make screeching noises for sudden brakings and other travel adventures.

PART 3
Three to Six Months

Games of Laughter

So, you've made it three months. Congratulations! This is where the fun really begins. What a thrill when your baby begins to coo to you or smile when you appear at her crib and you realize she's becoming a real little person. She can also appreciate a few toys—musical stuffed animals, rubber rings for chewing, or, a real favorite, your dark glasses! You'll be surprised for how long she can entertain herself while you start the wash or help an older child with a puzzle. We were able to grab a few free moments to unload the dishwasher or make a quick phone call by letting Amy keep Kate company in her big playpen. An older brother or sister can squeak toys, shake rattles, and wind up the musical lamb or mobile with enough enthusiasm to stretch out a baby's playtime so she takes an extra long nap!

Soon your baby will laugh right out loud. Once we heard Kate's deep chuckle, we couldn't get enough of it. Many of the following games were designed to encourage laughing, by tickling, kissing, or surprising an unsuspecting baby! So, come on and have a few laughs.

9
Shadow Shapes

Purpose: To help the baby learn to follow moving objects with her eyes

Equipment: Sunlit wall or small, bright light. This game was discovered when Kate decided five A.M. was a dandy time to wake up. As the sun rose, bright sunlight flooded one wall, casting all kinds of distinct shadows.

Position: Place the baby in her infant seat facing the wall or over your shoulder so she can try to touch the wall shadows (this is best), or lay her down with her head turned toward the wall.

Procedure:
1. Lift the baby up over your shoulder, perhaps encouraging a burp, and lean back so most of her weight is against you. This way you can free one hand to hold up in the light.
2. Holding your hand so that it casts a clean shadow on the wall, wiggle your fingers, open and close your hand.

155

3. You may not have the expertise to make lions, dogs, rabbits, cows, or birds, but your baby won't care. Just so long as it moves and wiggles, it will captivate her interest. I worked hard on my bunny and was quite proud of it, but there always seemed to be something wrong with one ear and it never did have a tail! But Kate thought it was great.

Variation: Hold up an object that casts a clear shadow; a comb, spoon, or flower.

Suggestion: If possible, hold your hand or object back out of baby's sight so she can only see the shadow.

Including More Players: You really could use a partner in this game so you arms don't get so tired! Amy made beautiful sweeping motions all across the wall for Kate's eyes to follow. Julie also had Amy count the number of fingers she held up or took away, making Shadow Shapes a sophisticated counting game as well as a visual game for Kate.

10
Indian Chants

Purpose: To encourage verbal development
To show the baby she has control over sounds and environment
To stimulate sense of hearing

Equipment: None

Position: Game is best played when the baby is lying down on her back and you are leaning over her. A good diaper-changing game!

Procedure:
1. Hold one of the baby's hands in yours and place it over your mouth as you sound one long, low-pitched, "Ahhhhhh."
2. Pat the baby's hand on and off your mouth so the two of you are making an Indian chantlike song.
3. Change the level of your voice, high and low, as baby's hand continues to pat your mouth.
4. Make a variety of vowel sounds to change the rhythm.
5. If the baby begins to "talk," try to pat her hand over her own mouth.

This is something that may happen the first time you play or not until several rounds later.

Including More Players: This game also lends itself to including a big brother or sister. You can take turns chanting the baby's mouth if each of you hold a hand and take turns patting it on your mouth. This way the baby will turn her head from side to side to follow the sound. Or an older child can simply chant on her own to entertain the baby. Amy, not a very passive observer as you've probably noticed, danced to her own chants while Kate watched her with unabashed admiration.

159

11
Horsie Bucks

Purpose: To teach a baby that bouncy, slightly scary play can be fun
To give a baby not sitting up yet a chance to view the world from a different angle

Equipment: None

Position: Lie on your back with your knees drawn up. Place the baby on your stomach in a sitting position, facing you, as if she were riding a horse. Hold her sides firmly. You may want to put a pillow under your head so you can see what's going on!

Procedure: 1. Once the baby is settled on your stomach, say, "Hey, Kate! You want to go for a horsie ride?" Raise your stomach up (lifting up the baby) and say, "Up! Do you like to go up?"
2. Lower your stomach, saying, "Down! Now Kate is down."
3. Repeat this procedure several times and, if she enjoys it, go on to step 4.

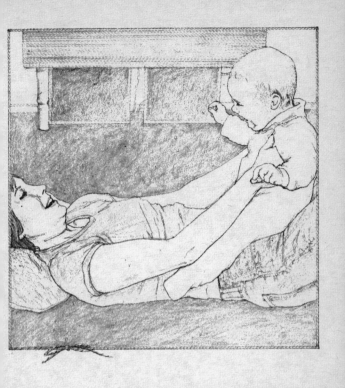

4. Pick up the pace a little, bouncing the baby up and down. Singing or chanting anything at this point is a good trick as the baby is bouncing most of the air out of your lungs, but if you can manage a "Look at Kate ride her horsie!" she'll enjoy it.

5. Change the pace after a while. Lift the baby up and down once, stop briefly, then go up and down twice, quickly. Surprise bounces often sent Kate into real giggles!

Suggestion: This game can wear a younger baby out, so watch for signs of frustration and limit time to about ten minutes.

Including More Players: Anyone under the age of nine or ten may have difficulty with this game, making it unsafe. But a toddler or even three or four year old will like to try her chances with Horsie Bucks. But you've got to have the stomach for it! Amy was a bit disappointed in the ride, though —not fast enough—and was told to wait until Daddy gets home. He was thrilled, right?

12

Pounce!

Purpose: To teach the baby to anticipate sudden changes with pleasure, to enjoy a surprise

Equipment: None

Position: Put the baby on her back, or sit her in an infant's seat.

Procedure:
1. Place your hands along the baby's sides or arms, so as to avoid startling her.
2. Lean over the baby's face.
3. Quickly change your normal, pleasant expression to one of wide-eyed surprise and open-mouthed astonishment. Accompany the changed expression with a gasp, a "Huh!", in a loud whisper.
4. Relax your face.
5. Repeat the shocked look and indrawn breath.
6. Relax your face again. Babies love surprises, and the repeat show should get a laugh out of the baby.

She'll be watching, now. Are you going to do that trick again?

7. Do it again. And again.

Variation: For a baby closer to six months, introduce a little bit of a jerk or pounce into the action.

Including More Players: Before Amy could play this wonderful, harmless game with Katie, she had to practice changing her expression, using the bathroom mirror. Of course, making faces at yourself in the mirror is a full-time activity on its own, as any teenager can testify!

13
Tickle Time

Purpose: To acquaint the baby with the features of her face

To give an older sibling the chance to touch the new baby's face in a positive, loving way under mother's guidance

Equipment: Sofa

Position: Mother holds the baby against her shoulder.

Procedure:
1. Mother takes the baby's hand in hers and guides it around her own face and under her chin.
2. Mother says, "Tickle! Tickle! Katie, you're tickling me!" Giggle.
3. Then guide the baby's hand along your face and arms.
4. Now it's your turn. Say, "I'm going to tickle you, Katie!" Gently touch the baby's forehead, cheeks, and nose. Say, "Does that tickle? Is Mommy tickling you, Katie?"

Suggestions: Be sure anyone playing has clean hands and clipped fingernails—especially the

165

baby. Hair, grabbed in the fist of a determined baby, can be most quickly and painlessly released by peeling back those flexible baby fingers! Play this game as long as the little player is happy.

Variation: Let the baby lie on the bed while you lean over her.

Including More Players: This game gives the older child an excellent chance to touch and feel the baby. While you hold the baby, guide her hands to "tickle" the older child's face and arms. Then, let the older child "tickle" the baby by touching under her chin and along her arms. Adapt your dialogue to include the older child, saying, "Amy's tickling Katie!"

14

Tell Me About It

Purpose: To encourage verbalization

Equipment: None

Position: Let the baby lie on her back on a quilt or sit her in her infant seat.

Procedure:

1. The baby initiates this game by cooing or blowing noisy bubbles. You pick up on the sound, saying, "Why, what's that story all about, Katie? Tell me that story!"

2. Mimic the sound the baby made. This gets her going more. She mimics you, and then you mimic her.

3. Ask the baby questions, using words she hears every day. "Did Daddy tell you that story?" "Is that what happened to your bottle?"

Variation: An older child can introduce this game to the baby. When I heard Katie "talking" in her crib, I said to Amy, "Go talk to Katie; Katie needs someone to talk to." "But Katie doesn't know *how* to

talk!'' Amy replied. "Well, you have to go talk to her, so she will learn. Like this." At this point you show the older child how to mimic and question the baby.

Suggestion: Play at your own risk! Amy taught Katie a terrible piercing shriek to which the diners at the cafeteria at Sequoia National Park were unexpectedly treated one summer night. One minute Katie was sitting peacefully in her seat on the table, then it was *Eek!* and all forks dropped!

15
Laugh-in

Purpose: To get the baby to laugh out loud. Also, if you have an overticklish baby, she needs to become less sensitive, and we accomplish this with Laugh-in.

Equipment: None

Position: Lay the baby on her back on a quilt, and lean over her.

Procedure:
1. You know how to make a raspberry noise, don't you? Just fill up your mouth with air and blow. Try it on your own arm—leave your mouth open a little bit—feel that vibration? Babies adore being given the raspberry! Try it on her bare tummy. Get a giggle?
2. Go for the armpit. Katie gets a chuckle from this.
3. Soles of her feet? Back of her neck?

Variation: Kissing is a first cousin of the raspberry; the vibration, though more subtle, makes a nice change.

Suggestions: Don't overdo it. You don't want to make the baby hysterical. Get a routine going, hit the same spots in a repeat pattern. But ten minutes is plenty.

Including More Players: When Amy tried this, bubbles foamed out of her mouth. But she enjoyed doing "wasbewies" on Vickie, her doll.

16

Hands Down!

Purpose: To develop eye-hand coordination
To help the baby "track" moving objects with her eyes

Equipment: None

Position: Put the baby on your lap, facing front.

Procedure:
1. Put your hands, backs up, on the baby's lap.
2. Hope the baby will slap at your hands. If not, take her hands and put them on top of yours.
3. Slide your hands out from under the baby's, and put them on top of hers. Say, "My hands are on top of yours!"
4. Now, take the baby's hands and gently slap them down on top of yours.
5. Repeat step 3.
6. Repeat step 4. At first, the baby won't be very adept at this game. But you'll be surprised at how well she'll be able to play a month from now!

Suggestion: Start the game very early. By the time the baby is six months of age, Hands Down! could be a lifesaver in a restaurant. At least, she's grabbing your hands and not your knife and fork.

Including More Players: Let the baby lie on her quilt on the rug while the other child lies (tummy down) facing her. Teach them how to play, and then watch while you're getting dinner ready. Remember—gently, gently!

17
Bug Patrol

Purpose: To help develop eye-hand coordination. A baby that's just about to create a scene can have her attention diverted. The tapping gets 'em.

Equipment: None

Position: Have the baby sitting in a high chair or on the floor—anywhere that has a hard, flat surface to play on.

Procedure:
1. Run your fingers quickly across the surface in front of her, tapping your nails noisily.
2. Say, "Here comes the bug! Scurry, scurry, scurry!" Run your first two fingers in quick succession across her hands.
3. Say, "Try to catch the bug!"
4. Run the bug up the baby's arm and under her neck. (See the game Mousie in *Games Babies Play*.)
5. Let the baby catch your fingers. Say, "Oh, you got the bug. Katie got the bug!"

Suggestions: Remember this quickie in a restaurant—you'll be glad you've got it at your fingertips! A word of warning, though—attention spans (yours and baby's) aren't long with Bug Patrol, sad to say.

Including More Players: Amy and Katie played the game together, and Amy, bored with fingers, got a little windup bug she could scoot across the table in front of Katie. Older siblings will create bugs of their own—but theirs are harder to catch!

18

Hop on Pop

(Courtesy of Dr. Seuss)

Purpose: To strengthen the baby's leg muscles and encourage the giggles. (This game has benefits for the adult player, too. It will tighten the tummy, and help shed unwelcome flab, guaranteed.)

Equipment: None

Position: Daddy lies on his back on the floor, head supported by a pillow. He holds the baby on his stomach in a standing position with his hands under her armpits, supporting her.

Procedure:
1. Bounce baby from her standing position on your stomach. (Not too high, at first!)
2. As she's bouncing say, "Stop! You must not hop on top of pop!"
3. Repeat the bouncing and the protesting, as long as your stomach holds out!

Including
More Players: Let the older child lie next to you, and
with her doll or stuffed animal join in
with, "Stop! You must not hop!" My
husband Jerry, who now has a cast-iron
stomach, lets Amy, age three, play with
him—but not after dinner!

177

19

Go for the Toe

Purpose: To limber up baby's legs
To make the baby aware of her own body, and her own feelings

Equipment: None

Position: Put the baby on her back on the floor. Sit close by.

Procedure:
1. Gently encourage the baby to bring one big toe (foot, too) up to your hands. Say, "Go for that toe, Kate!"
2. Bring the toe close to her mouth. Say, "There's your toe! That's part of you, Katie!" Let's face it—most babies love to suck on their toes; you wouldn't want yours to miss out on this, would you, just for lack of a little guidance? Surely I don't have to mention only *clean* toes used here, please.
3. Bring up the other foot and put it in her other hand. Looks hard? It's easy as pie for a baby! Say, "Now you've got all ten toes. Go, go for the toe!"

Variation: A really with-it mother tickles the bottoms of baby's feet, for added fun.

Suggestion: Most babies are naturally intrigued by their toes, but if your baby could care less, don't force it.

Including More Players: Older siblings should be carefully supervised if they are to play with the baby. A baby is limber, but not that limber!

20

Bed Bouncies—Grandpa's Favorite

Purpose: To encourage the baby to laugh
To develop the baby's sense of balance

Equipment: A double bed is best, but a single bed or a daybed will do.

Position: Place the baby on her back on the bed and lean over her with your palms flat on the top of the bed on either side of her head, or at chest height.

Procedure:
1. With your hands, give the bed a series of little bounces—not too hard at first!
2. Say, "Look at Katie bounce! Look at that fat baby bounce!"
3. As soon as the baby begins to enjoy Bouncies, make them bigger— bounce her right off the bed and into the air!

Variation: When Kate could sit up well, Grandpa, with his long arms, would jiggle her, still sitting all across his big bed.

Suggestion: Not too soon after meals, Mommy!

Including With Katie propped on the pillows, Amy
More Players: would jump on all fours like a puppy at
the foot of the bed while Jerry and I
dressed to go out, keeping an eye on the
game of Bouncies being happily played
by the little sisters.

21

Neck Monster

Purpose: To encourage the baby to laugh out loud

Equipment: None

Position: Lay the baby on her back on the couch or carpet. Lean over the baby, supporting your weight on your hands on either side at the height of the baby's shoulders.

Procedure:
1. Starting at point A (the belly button), get your lips to point B (the neck) with a series of juicy kisses.
2. Don't give up until you've kissed that delicious spot where the double chins end and the neck begins. Getting to this point was quite a challenge with our roly-poly Kate!
3. Pause between attacks to give the baby a chance to catch her breath. Repeat the procedure, always going from A to B.

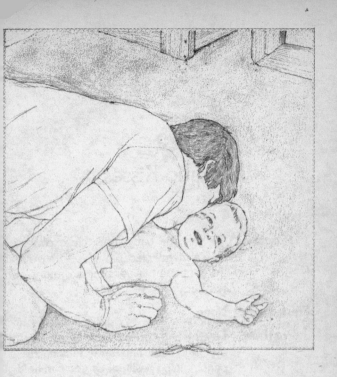

Variation: Roll the baby over and kiss up her back to that vulnerable spot on the back of her neck.

Suggestion: This is a great game at diaper-changing time. It takes the baby's mind off the fact that she has been laid ignominiously on her back. And, besides, *bare* is best!

Including More Players: We played this game with Amy when she was Katie's age, and to this day Amy flees, giggling wildly, from Jerry, the Neck Monster, who chases her, growling, "I'm going to get that neck!"

22

Eskimo Kisses

Purpose: To give the baby more close contact with a friendly face
To continue her awareness of parts of her body

Equipment: None

Position: Lay the baby on her back as you bend over her—you know, the familiar diaper changing position! Or you can hold her out in front of you while you sit or stand.

Procedure:
1. First snuggle your face up to the baby's, saying, "How about a big kiss, Katie?" Follow this up with your juiciest, squeakiest kiss on her cheek or neck.
2. Now introduce the classic Eskimo kiss saying, "Here's a new way to kiss, Kate!" Rub your noses together. This usually got a chuckle out of Kate. Imagine how silly it must appear to a baby—rubbing noses. What will they think of next?

3. Repeat steps 1 and 2, comparing the more conventional kisses with the Eskimo kisses.

4. As you rub noses, say, "Nose, Kate, we are touching noses!" Stop and encourage her to feel your nose and hers by guiding her hands.

Suggestion: Instead of the usual kiss goodnight or bye-bye at the baby-sitter's, try giving a quick Eskimo kiss - saying, "Bye-bye! Here's an Eskimo kiss!"

Including More Players: Amy adored the spontaneous surprise of getting an Eskimo kiss good night and enjoyed showing Kate the difference

185

between the two kisses. The best way to let an older child give kisses is to hold the baby on your lap while the older child "kisses" her. This way the children are on the same level and it minimizes strain on the baby's neck!

PART 4
Six to Nine Months

Games of Interaction

After the first three to six months in which the baby was relatively immobile, the next few months come as quite a shock. Babies don't have to be proficient at crawling to get themselves from here to there. Kate's first mode of transportation was creeping along backward on her tummy. It's rather unnerving to return from answering the telephone and discover that the spot where you left your baby is now empty! Then, upon closer inspection of the scene, you find she scooted under the coffee table! Kate was forever backing up into the fireplace, the dirtiest spot in the house, right? Of course she couldn't see where she was going and I really think she had her eye on the coffee table but couldn't make herself go in that direction. Amy thought it was great and made many grand announcements, "Kate's in the fireplace, *again!*" if she even so much as looked in its direction.

Suddenly your baby can make things happen instead of things just happening to her. In the next three months, first by sitting, then creeping, crawling, pulling to stand, and perhaps even by walking, your baby will be determined to investigate her world. And so she should!

Another facet of your baby's interest in the world is her rediscovery of the people around her. Not so much what they look like—her first big interest—but what they do! For this is also the age of imitation. Try playing some old favorites now, like Peek-a-boo and Pat-a-cake (*Games Babies Play*). Katie watched Amy, fascinated by anything she did. A big brother or sister can be a vital teacher at this stage. When trying to cook dinner, get out the pots, pans, and wooden spoons. Katie caught on very quickly watching Amy bang away.

The following are our favorite six to nine month games of interaction and imitation. They are designed to help you and your family enjoy the lively little explorer!

23
Cheerleading

Purpose: To exercise arms, limber up the tummy Also, this game teaches imitation

Equipment: None

Position: Sit on the floor facing the baby. Hold the baby's wrists, one in each hand.

Procedure:
1. Raise the baby's hands above her head, all the way up. Now, lower her arms. Repeat. Say, "Rah! Rah! Sis! Boom! Bah!"
2. Hold the baby's arms out sideways. Say, "Two-four-six-eight! Who do we appreciate?"
3. Raise the baby's hands back above her head and say, "Katie! K! K!"
4. Katie especially loved having her hands rolled over each other, and to be made to clap her hands above her head.

Variations: Make up your own cheers—personalize them—as in, "Give me a K, give me a K! Give me an A! A! A!" (Continue until you've spelled out the baby's name.)

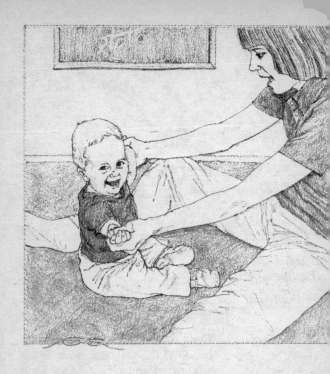

***Including
More Players:*** This was wonderful motivation for Amy to leap around the room singing, "Give me an A . . ." Those of us who have tried and failed at Jumping Jacks will appreciate the good practice this game gives in those difficult motor skills—plus there's a little spelling practice on the side!

24
Tiger Roar

Purpose: To encourage verbal imitation—
pretalking skills

Equipment: None

Position: Place the baby in a high chair, in a ca[r] seat, or on the floor.

Procedure:
1. Say "I'm going to roar like a tiger Grrrr!" (Not too loud, not too close to the baby's face.)
2. Repeat roar and then say, "You[r] turn, Katie—you be the tiger."
3. Of course, the baby may not pick up on the rules of the game right away and roar back at once, so just try again. The baby will catch on.

Suggestions: If the loud noise frightens the baby, stop the roar and stick to simple sounds. Save the meows and oinks, obviously the next step, until later.

Including More Players: This is a great game for an older child, as long as she does not roar too loudly. Amy had fun prowling around Katie while teaching her to "roar." She even pinned a newspaper tail to her pants!

25
Human Jungle Gym
(Part I)

Purpose: To strengthen leg and arm muscles
To practice climbing, pulling to stand

Equipment: None

Position: Lay on your side on the floor or bed.
Place the baby in a crawling position
beside your legs or hips.

Procedure:
1. Call to your baby, "Come on, Kate.
   Can you climb up on me?" Pull her
   up so she is kneeling with her hands
   holding onto your legs.
2. Encourage her to "climb," holding
   onto your pants or shirt, by gently
   lifting her to stand as she holds onto
   you.
3. If your baby is already pulling up on
   things on her own, she will enjoy
   grabbing your shirt, pants, and even
   your hair, to climb up on you. Kate
   liked to climb up and catapult right
   over to the other side!

Variation: Kate took this game one step further as she pulled up on people *standing* near her. She soon learned that nightgowns couldn't be trusted, too swishy, but blue jeans were just right.

Suggestion: Teach this game at your own risk. Babies enjoy it so much that soon it's no longer safe to lie on the rug to watch television or read. You'll be attacked by the Human Jungle Gym climber!

Including
More Players: Amy enjoyed Human Jungle Gym but found it difficult to hold still as Kate "climbed" her. The game usually turned into wrestling—one of Amy's favorites with her daddy—but still a bit rough for Kate. An older child may enjoy being the standing target when your baby begins to pull up on legs, but be sure to teach the older one to lower the baby down *before* walking away!

26
My Name's Red!

Purpose: To entertain the baby and show her the fun of surprises

Equipment: A doll hand puppet is best—one with a face and hair—but any puppet animal or monster will do.

Procedure:

1. Slip doll puppet on your hand and begin a conversation with your baby. We had a doll with bright red yarn pigtails, a red polka-dot dress and big blue eyes. We called her Red and gave her a Southern accent. She started each conversation the same way: "Hi, y'all! My name's Red!" Red would pat Katie and say, "Are you Katie?"

2. Make the puppet get right up close to your baby so she can touch it. Red used to put her face right next to Kate's and swish her hair around. Kate would grab the red yarn and pull Red toward her. We would then have Red squeal for help: "Help, help! This baby's got a hold of my

beautiful red hair!" I would rescue Red by unclenching Kate's grip.

3. Let the puppet play peek-a-boo, pat-a-cake, or lie still and jump up like a jack-in-the-box for the baby. Ham it up as a silly puppet.

Variation: Your baby might enjoy wearing a puppet. Small finger puppets are fun and fit tiny hands better.

Including More Players: An older child will enjoy talking to your puppet. Red would ask Amy her name, where she went to pre-school, the name of her favorite book, and so forth. Amy always answered very seriously—

197

looking right at Red instead of the puppeteer! A good way to get the older child's feelings about the baby out in the open is to have the puppet complain about the baby, saying, "Does that baby ever pull your hair? What do you do? Does she get into your toys?" Amy used to be very defensive, saying, "Well, she's just a baby and doesn't know any better." (Wonder where she heard that?) After discussing the baby, let the puppet jump on the older child's head or back and say, "Let's wrestle!" You don't want to get too serious in discussing the baby. Keep it light, voicing what you think the older child may be feeling, then back to some fun games for the baby. Naming parts of the body, singing, and tickling are all good puppet games for children of all ages.

27

Cupboard of Fun

Purpose: To encourage the baby to investigate her environment
To further develop small-muscle coordination in the hands
To teach independent play

Equipment: A small cupboard or drawer in the kitchen (close to the floor) filled with plastic containers, lids, unbreakable bowls

Position: Place the baby next to the open cupboard or drawer.

Procedure:
1. As you begin cooking, say to the baby, "Look, this is your cupboard! What's in here?" If she is hesitant to explore, take one or two items out, putting them right next to her.
2. As the baby begins to reach into the drawer, or if she pulls something from the cupboard, praise her with a "Good girl! What did you find?" Name the object and then let her alone to continue her search.

3. If your baby has trouble getting involved in her cupboard and seems to want you to play too (you can usually tell because she will cling to your pants legs and whine), just keep busy going back and forth in the kitchen, encouraging her cheerfully to play. You can stop now and then and show her a new treasure from the cupboard, but keep moving and soon she'll get the message and entertain herself. After all, you can't play games *all* the time, right?

4. When everything has been taken out, show her how you put things back. If she is still interested, start over. Katie used to try to get into the cupboard after it had been emptied, as if this were the ultimate goal of the game!

Including More Players: Amy got a real kick out of this game. One, because it was fun to have a big mess in the kitchen and two, because she enjoyed showing Kate how each thing worked or what it was for. The first time you "play" this, set up a system like we did: Kate pulled some treasure out of the cupboard and studied it for a few moments. When she had discarded it, Amy picked it up, showed her what it was for (mixing, stirring), and then sorted it into the proper place. Soon Amy had all the lids together, all the bowls, cups, or spoons each in their own pile. When the cupboard was empty and Katie turned to Amy's neat piles, everything had to go back into the cupboard again to start over.

28
Amy's Own Peek-a-boo

Purpose:	To help the baby learn to anticipate another player's actions
Equipment:	None
Position:	Have the baby sit on the floor in front of you with her back to you. Kneel about a foot behind her.
Procedure:	1. Lean over so that your cheek is close to the baby's right cheek, your heads side-by-side, and say, "Peek-a-boo!"
	2. Draw back, wait a few seconds, and do the same thing on the other side.
	3. Repeat step 1.
	4. Now watch from your position behind her which way the baby is turning her head. If she turns to the left, she obviously thinks you're going to repeat the pattern, so be sure you do. Don't disappoint the little darling!
	5. After a while—babies will play this for a long time—come right over the

top of her head for an upside-down face-to-face confrontation. This will really make her laugh!

Variation: As with the classic peek-a-boo game, you can hide behind a door or couch and pop out behind her.

Including More Players: Amy was the first one to play this game, sitting behind Katie and peeping around at her.

29
Gingerbread Man

Purpose: To encourage a beginning creeper in the fine art of crawling

Equipment: Balloon (optional)

Position: Put the baby on her hands and knees—crawling position—and station yourself about a foot in front of her.

Procedure:
1. Begin to crawl slowly away in front of the baby, saying, "Come on, Katie, you can't catch me—I'm the Gingerbread Man!"
2. Katie always started right after us, because she was trying to catch those delicious-looking tennis shoes. Maybe you could tie a balloon to the leader's ankle to lure the baby after the Gingerbread Man.
3. Don't go too fast, or the baby will lose interest. The leader must stop just in front of the baby every now and then and let herself be caught!

Including More Players: This was one of Amy's favorites and a good game for an older child to play

with the baby. Once Katie could crawl with the speed of light, Amy took to running, whizzing past the baby, shouting, "You can't catch me—I'm the Gingerbread Man!" Katie would hustle right along after her, until flash! Amy whizzes past again. This was more than enough of a thrill for Katie. One time Katie came plodding around a corner unexpectedly and startled Amy—then Amy screamed. Amy pretended the fox had gotten her—Katie didn't even know she was playing.

30
Be My Echo

Purpose: To encourage verbalization
To introduce new sounds into the baby's "vocabulary"

Equipment: None

Position: Put the baby in a car seat or high chair.

Procedure:
1. Make a series of simple sounds, such as "la, la, la." Encourage the baby to answer back, by saying, "Be my echo. Sing what I sing!"
2. Now, take a sound the baby already makes—like Katie's "da, da, da, da"—and sing it like a scale—high to low, and back again. Encourage the baby to echo you.
3. Repeat steps 1 and 2; repetition is what makes the game work.
4. In desperate cases, where the baby doesn't echo your sounds, you imitate her. Say, "I'll be your echo. I'll sing what you sing." She'll love it.

Variations: Now that the basic work is done, the fun begins. Take the baby for a walk, and if

you find one of those barely finished houses, play Be My Echo inside, for a thrilling effect. Tunnels are fun, too. We have walked through a tunnel with Amy going "Ah, ah, ah," listening to the echo; blocks later and well out of the tunnel, there will be Katie, jouncing in the back pack, going, "Ah, ah, ah."

Including More Players: Be My Echo makes an ideal car game, with the older child making the sound for the baby to copy. Older children like leading in this game, as in pat-a-cake.

31

Roller Coaster Ride

Purpose: To help the baby enjoy an exciting game

Equipment: None

Position: Sit far back on a sofa with feet braced against a sturdy coffee table. Put the baby on your stomach, using your knees and the top part of your legs as a sort of back rest.

Procedure:
1. Say, "Click! Click! Click!", imitating the sound the wheels of the roller coaster make getting the cars up to the top of the first steep hill.
2. Say, "Phew! Down you go!", swaying from side to side. Hold the baby, and when you sway from side to side, make deep dips.
3. Repeat. "Click! Click! Phew! Down we go!"

Including More Players: Amy saw the Matterhorn Ride on television; that's how we made up the game. When she played, Katie sat on my chest

and Amy sat on my stomach. Amy held
Katie just as if it were a real roller
coaster. Amy loved it, but in real life I
don't think we'd get her near such a
scary ride! You can even pretend to
strap the children in to make it more
authentic.

32
Rolling Along

Purpose: To develop baby's balancing ability
To develop overall large-motor coordination

Equipment: An inflatable, cylindrical baby toy (found through Sears catalogue) filled with colorful balls or bells, or a cylindrical pillow (like the bolster found at the end of a sofa)

Position: Sit on the floor with the baby and let her touch, squeeze, bite, or hug the cylinder. Let her find out what noise it makes, if any, or what it is. Once the baby is familiar with the new toy, begin the game.

Procedure:
1. Gently lay the baby, tummy down, on top of the cylinder, feet pushing against the ground.
2. Slowly roll the baby on top of the cylinder, until her hands are touching the floor in front of her. Kate instinctively put her hands out in front of her, but if your baby does not, by all means show her how!

3. Turn her around and place her in a kneeling position, hands on top of cylinder, as you hold it steady. Encourage her to climb up on it, either verbally or with a little boost!

4. Repeat as long as everyone enjoys the game.

Variation: Your toy can also be used as a ball and rolled back and forth between players.

Suggestion: Be sure to familiarize your baby with the new toy before beginning, but if the game frightens her, of course, save it for next month. Sometimes that floating feeling can give a baby the creeps!

Including More Players: I suppose I really must admit it—our toy split a seam during one of Amy's demonstrations for Kate. But it had held up through a lot of rough play and cost under five dollars, so it was well worth it! We don't recommend an older child "roll" the baby, but rather be a demonstrator.

33
Row-a-Boat

Purpose: To give the baby a sense of timing
To strengthen the baby's stomach muscles

Equipment: None

Position: Sit on the floor with your legs straight out in front of you. Place baby in the same position, facing you. Baby's legs should be inside yours.

Procedure:
1. Hold both of baby's hands in yours.
2. Slowly lean back, gently pulling the baby so she leans toward you.
3. Begin to sing, "Row, row, row your boat, gently down the stream. . . ."
4. Lean forward, gently pushing the baby backward.
5. Continue to lean back and forth until baby catches on to the rhythm.

Suggestion: Katie loved leaning forward while I leaned back, but wasn't too crazy about leaning back herself! Actually this worked out better because I would lean way back and then sit up—great for *my*

214

tummy!—then gently lean Katie back just a bit!

Including More Players: Actually this game is better suited to be played between children because they are closer to the same size. However, you need to supervise so the older child doesn't "row" the baby too vigorously.

34
Where's That Kate?

Baby's First Hide-and-Seek

Purpose: To stimulate a bored baby
To establish a base for learning a more complex game later

Equipment: Baby walker

Position: Place the baby in the walker

Procedure: When fixing dinner or doing the laundry, your baby in her walker may begin to fuss. Instead of reaching for a cracker, try this:

1. On the way to the refrigerator or laundry room, give your baby a push along the way.
2. Whisk her around a corner, under the stairs or behind a big plant.
3. Call to her from where you are. "Where's that Kate? Where's she hiding?"
4. On your way back from the laundry room (a matter of minutes) "find" your baby. Say, "Oh! There you are!"

5. Return her to the original spot where you are working.

6. On your next trip down the hall "hide" your baby again—only to discover her on your return trip!

Suggestions: Be sure you only leave your baby hidden for a few minutes. This is a good game to play while house cleaning or vacuuming since you're up walking from place to place anyway!

Including More Players: An older child will enjoy this game, and the baby is quite safe in her walker. In fact, Amy made the game easier—she did the hiding (delighting in finding new spots) and I did the finding! But be prepared to seek out a hiding big brother or sister once in a while or even take a turn hiding yourself!

PART 5
Nine to Twelve Months

Action Games

Nine months have passed and your baby has turned the corner and is coming down the homestretch toward her first birthday—fast! We think this is a delightful age—at least it starts out that way. Your baby, having mastered crawling, can now concentrate on where to go and what to do with this amazing skill. Kate spent much of her time finding tiny pieces of fluff on the carpet or minute crumbs in the kitchen. Quite pleased with herself, she would offer them up to me. Yet, just as I would reach out—pop!—into the mouth!

When it is very quiet in the house and your baby is not in sight you'd better check the bathroom—is the toilet paper all unrolled? I thought so! Was the lid down on the toilet? I hope so! When our bathroom was empty, the next place to check was Amy's room. Whenever Kate discovered that door open it was Christmas-come-early!

Games can now take on a new dimension. Your

baby will begin to understand simple commands, remember the structure of a game, and may even initiate the play herself. Music should be reemphasized as your baby can sway her head, bounce up and down, or even try to sing along.

This is an active period in which your baby will be filled with confidence in her physical abilities. Watch how proud she is as she "walks" across the room on her tiptoes, holding your hands. An older child can easily be shown how to slowly "walk" the baby and then they can both feel quite pleased with themselves. Cheer your baby on, be generous with your praise—the more confident she is the easier it will be for her to take those first few steps (and stumbles!) on her own!

It's sometimes hard for a baby this age to wind down and go to sleep. We found that having a bedtime book kept Katie in touch with books as well as signaled to her that this was the time for quiet and rest.

35
Hide 'n' Boo

Purpose: To teach the baby to accept surprises

Equipment: None

Position: The adult player crouches on all fours
behind a couch or a big chair. The baby
is in a crawling position out of sight
around the corner on the other side of
the piece of furniture.

Procedure: 1. Get into position, and call the baby
by name. "Katie! Katie! Where's
Mommy? Come and find Mom-
my!"
2. If the baby remains motionless (baf-
fled!), peek around the corner, and
pull your head right back, as soon as
the baby glimpses you.
3. Call again—this'll start her scram-
bling your way!
4. Just as the baby gets to the corner,
spring out on all fours, and say,
"Boo!"
5. Give the baby a hug, and put her
back in her original spot. Go quickly

back to your hiding place, and call
again.

6. This time, the baby will know it's a
game, scuttle around the corner,
grinning, knowing you're going to
spring out and say, "Boo!" Do so.

7. For the third round of Hide 'n' Boo,
let the baby come all the way
around the corner, then fall back,
throw up your arms, and exclaim,
"Oh! You found me!"

Variation: Change your hiding spot as baby gets
older and more familiar with the game.
Around the side of a bed is a good place

to play, or between rooms, around a wall.

Including More Players:

1. Amy usually didn't sit still long enough for Katie to get to her hiding place—she always met Katie halfway, shrieking, "Boo!"

2. An adult can hide with the baby, calling to the older child, "Amy! Come, find us!" Then you have to act surprised as the older child whips around the corner. "Oh! You *found* us!"

36
Baby Basketball

Purpose: To develop large-muscle coordination
To give some background experience in a basic game

Equipment: There are many variations on this game. The equipment can range from a wicker clothes hamper, wastebasket, or playhouse window, to an actual child-sized basketball game (Fisher-Price makes an excellent one). If you improvise the "basket," you'll also need small balls, bean bags, or blocks for the "ball."

Position: Set up your "basket" a few feet away from the seated baby.

Procedure:
1. Getting down on the baby's level, crawl over to the basket and drop the ball into it. Repeat, saying, "Look, Kate! I made a basket!"
2. Hand a ball to the baby, saying, "Can Kate make a basket? Go on, drop it in!" If she is reluctant to do

so, encourage her by walking her over to the basket.

3. Take your turn again and then let your baby try it again.

Variations: Santa brought Amy a basketball game for Christmas and it was on that that we originally played our game. Kate, however, was the one who started dropping tennis balls into the clothes hamper and then blocks into Amy's playhouse windows! And I didn't figure out she had played a solo game with the wastebasket until I emptied the trash and out fell two Ping-Pong balls and a bean bag!

Suggestion: Sometimes a baby will sit watching intently but makes no move to join in. Continue to demonstrate a few more times. More than likely as soon as you leave her alone she'll creep over and try her luck!

Including More Players: This is where an older child comes in very handy! A baby will imitate just about anything a big brother or sister does, so just set them up and leave them alone—a chance to finally read the Sunday paper!

37
Attack!—Daddy's Favorite

Purpose: To show how anticipation of the surprise is half the fun

To encourage the baby to initiate part of the game herself

Equipment: None

Position: Place the baby in a sitting position five to seven feet from you. Kneel, facing the baby.

Procedure:
1. Crawl slowly toward the baby, bringing your hands down dramatically hard as you go. Say, "I'm coming in for an attack! Here I come to get Kate!" (You are stalking your prey.)
2. Just before you get to the baby, lower your head and quickly, but gently, bump it into the baby's tummy. Katie delighted in this ending and would grab on to Jerry's head, squealing with satisfaction.
3. Return to the original position and repeat the "stalk" and "attack" steps.

4. After a few rounds of this, we found Kate couldn't wait to be attacked and she took the initiative to attack us! Starting seven or eight feet away, stalk the baby slowly. Then when you are still a few feet away, lower your head and encourage your baby to attack you—call her if necessary.

5. Once she understands her role, to play the game all you have to do is watch for her to make her moves as you stalk toward her. Then, put your head down as she rushes up! But watch it—Kate would rush up and climb right over our heads!

Suggestion: Sound effects help build the fun and anticipation.

Including
More Players: This game is not ideal for a young child (under five) to play with a baby brother or sister. We all know how babies pull hair—and it does hurt! Also there's the risk of bumping heads as the attackee rushes up to the attacker. So, supervise carefully, or better yet, play while the older child is at preschool or watching *Sesame Street!*

38
Bzzzt!

Purpose: To encourage laughter
To distract the baby who has had an unhappy experience (fallen down, or run into something)

Equipment: None

Position: Any position is fine. The baby can be in a high chair, car seat, or on the floor. She can also be standing.

Procedure:
1. Pointing an index finger at the baby, make a "bzzzt!" sound, and zero in like a corkscrew to a ticklish spot on her tummy.
2. Zero in on another spot, on the opposite side.
3. Then come around to zero in on the back of the baby's neck, or the middle of her back.
4. By this time, she'll be chortling away, happy again. Repeat all three spots. You can even say, "I'm coming to get you!"

Variation: Once the baby is on to the game, try a surprise "bzzzt!" out of order: instead of side-side-back, zero in side-*back*-side!

Suggestion: This is a good game to play if you are a stranger to the baby and want to get acquainted.

Including More Players: This is an easy game to learn, with guaranteed quick results. In fact, toddlers love to squeal and run from an unexpected game of Bzzzt! when initiated by Mom or Dad!

39
Drrrrop, Plop!

Purpose: To have some silly, slightly scary, fun

Equipment: None

Position: Stand up, holding the baby close against your shoulder with both hands.

Procedure:
1. Stretch out your arms, holding the baby in front of you, and slowly lower her, saying, "Drrrrop."
2. At the last minute (when she's about waist high in your arms), say, "Plop!" and loosen your grip slightly so she slips in the air for a second before you retighten your hold.
3. Repeat steps 1 and 2 a few times.
4. If the baby is enjoying the game (lots of giggles), try a change of pace after the "Drrrrop." Katie loved a surprise attack of three or four "Plops" in a row after the initial "Drrrrop!"

Variation: For a more timid baby try a slow motion version. After the slow descent of "Drrrrop," gently swing the baby down

in your arms as you bend down for that final "Plop."

Suggestion: We don't recommend Drrrrop, Plop! right after meals, but it works wonders on a baby with a pinched finger or stepped-on toe.

40
Go Ball, Go!

Purpose: To exercise large-motor skills
To further develop eye-hand coordina
tion

Equipment: Two balls no smaller than softballs (
larger than volleyballs. The balls shou'
be of different colors or sizes.

Position: This game requires a third player, so l
your older child (or an adult) in on th
fun! Sit on the floor with the baby :
your lap; the older child sits opposi'
you about five feet away.

Procedure: 1. To start, use one ball. Roll it towar
your older child and have her roll
back. Hold your baby's hands :
yours so she can "catch" the ba
and "roll" it back to big sister!

2. Introduce the second ball. The olde
child holds one ball; you and th
baby hold the other. Say, "On
two, three, go ball, go!" and ro
your ball to the older child while sh
rolls her ball to you.

234

3. In the event the balls should bump, which inevitably they will, let your baby and older child chase after them—adding excitement to the game.

4. After several "bumps," Amy became annoyed with having to chase after the ball—being a serious ball player at three and a half! So, we devised a system to avoid bumps. Having one small ball and another larger one, we decided that the small ball would be tossed, while the larger ball would be rolled.

5. Count "One, two, three, go ball,

go!'' and whoever is holding th
small ball tosses it over and th
player with the large ball (or blu
ball) rolls it. Amy enjoyed this cha
lenge, and Kate didn't know th
difference.

Variations: Quite by accident you'll find a numbe
of variations in this game. The ball ca
be bounced instead of rolled, it can g
under a chair between the two of you
or you can even try using three ball
Our games of Go Ball, Go! often ende
up differently each time we played!

Suggestion: If your baby tires of the game before th
older child does, have a spare ball and
wooden spoon handy. Your baby w
enjoy batting the ball around while yo
finish the game off with your older chil

41
Human Jungle Gym
(Part II)

Purpose: To enjoy some good rough and tumble fun

Equipment: None

Position: For this game you need a third player, preferably a child between two and five years. The adult player is on all fours, with her back legs straddled, and her back straight, thus forming a tunnel or bridge for the baby to play on or under.

Procedure:
1. Introduce the game by calling to the older child to crawl under the bridge. Tell her to weave in and out between your arms and legs, too.
2. Call to the baby to follow the older child—"Come on, Katie, follow Amy!"
3. Tell the older child she can crawl up onto the top of the bridge (adult's back). Amy then slithers, wriggling, down the other side, shouting, "Human jungle gym!"

4. Meanwhile, the baby continues t
crawl *under* the bridge.

5. Teach the older child to call ou
"Look out below!" and be caref
not to land on the baby!

Suggestion: This game can be as rough as you wan
to make it for the older child, keeping i
mind not to frighten the baby. A grea
game for a rainy day!

42
Can It!

Purpose: To develop a small-muscle coordination in the hand
To develop eye-hand coordination

Equipment: A one-pound coffee can (a sauce pan or high-sided bowl will do) and three Ping-Pong balls (best of all are those cat-toy balls with bells inside them)

Position: Place the little balls inside the can, and set it in front of the baby, who is sitting in a high chair or on the floor.

Procedure:
1. Pick up the can and say, "Look, Katie—look what's in the can! [Shake the can.] Can you get those out?" Hold the can out to the baby.
2. The baby will then reach in and attempt to get the balls out—can't imagine a baby that wouldn't! (Katie thinks it's food.) You can hold the baby's hand and help her get them out, of course.
3. Now, she's clutching the balls. Try to get her to put them back into the

239

can. But she doesn't want to give
them up! Hold out the can and say,
"Go ahead—put them back in!
Come on, Katie, put the balls back
there!" She'll finally plunk them
back in, you'll see.

4. Then, shake the can. Say, "There!
You put them back in—see? Now,
can you get them out again?" Offer
her the can.

5. "Oh, I get it," thinks the baby. "It's a
game!" Once she catches on to the
pattern, you won't have any trouble
getting her to put the balls back into
the can.

Variation:	Try a plastic cup and ice cubes!
Suggestion:	This is a good game for baby to play while Mom is cooking dinner. Just haul out her coffee can and kitty balls and you can concentrate on your cooking!
Including More Players:	Get another coffee can—kitty ball setup and let them "trade" balls—Amy always likes the looks of Katie's better than her own!

43

Tango for Two

Purpose: To continue your baby's appreciation of music

Equipment: Tango music—record, tape, or live

Position: Stand up and hold the baby in your arms; place your cheek against hers.

Procedure:
1. Hold your baby's left hand in your right hand, arms extended forward.
2. In a dramatic voice sing, "Da-dum, dum dum dum" while you march forward four steps, still cheek to cheek and arms outstretched—the classic tango position!
3. Turn your "partner" quickly around and "tango" back again—"Da-dum, dum dum dum!"
4. Continue back and forth several more times.

Variations: Katie loved the spin to turn around so much that we added a few extra twirls every now and then. Also, any music, your own or a record, works fine. If your

baby is enjoying herself, try a dip to really jazz things up!

Suggestion: This is a good distraction game, either to cheer up a bumped head or hold off a grumbling stomach until dinner is ready.

Including More Players: To involve an older brother or sister, let him or her take turns "tangoing" with you or, if possible, another grown-up could be their partner on the dance floor!

44

Airplane Ride

Purpose: To have some fast, exciting fun

Equipment: None

Position: Find a wide open area—preferably outdoors. Stand facing your baby and hold her hands in yours.

Procedure:
1. Turning around and around slowly lift your baby up off the ground so she is spinning straight out above the ground.
2. As you begin your spin, though, remember that this is an airplane ride! "Rrrrrr. . . . take off!" needs to accompany the initial spins.
3. Make about three turns and then gently lower her to the ground. Once again, as you bring the baby down for her landing, make it real! "Rrrr . . . touchdown."
4. Give her a big hug and check to see how she enjoyed the "ride."
5. If she is all smiles, up, up and away again!

Suggestion: Be sure you never spin around more than three or four times in a row. You never know when your baby will have had enough and it's disappointing for everyone when a good game goes sour.

Including More Players: This is an ideal beach game—lots of open space and soft sand to land in. We've made it into a real family affair—Jerry and I taking turns spinning Amy and Katie and then we all get hysterical watching Jerry trying to spin me or, even funnier, me spin him!

45

"Ring, Ring!"—Grandma's Favorite

Purpose: To encourage verbal development

Equipment: Two play telephones

Position: Sit facing the baby with your telephones at your sides.

Procedure:
1. Pretending to dial your baby, make your telephone ring, and also say, "Ring, ring. Ring, ring."
2. If your baby makes no move to pick up her phone, lift the receiver, hand it to her, and say, "Hi! Oh, hi Katie!"
3. Pretend to carry on a conversation. The game goes something like this: "Hi! Oh really? When? Oh! Well, okay. All right. Bye, bye!" If you try to talk too long, you're liable to be hung up on!
4. As you come to the end of your conversation, say, "Bye, bye" and hang up. Then tell your baby, "Say, 'Bye bye' " and help her hang up.

5. Repeat step 1. After my "Ring, ring" Katie would lift her receiver, clutch it to her chest, and squeal, "Hi!"

Variations: It's a good idea to keep a play phone near the real one. It never fails that as soon as you're on the phone, your baby needs something desperately. Hand her the play phone, smile at her, and make a lot of eye contact. As you talk to your caller, your baby just might be tricked into thinking you're playing with her!

Suggestions: Be flexible. If your baby crawls away from the phone, uninterested, just try the game some other time. If all she wants to do is pick up and hang up the receiver (yours too!), just go along with it. She'll soon want to play a more structured game with the telephone.

Including More Players: **1.** This game is obviously a natural for an older sibling. You can have your older child practice her telephone manners ("Who's calling, please?" and all that) while your baby goes along for the ride.
2. The play-phone-by-the-real-phone strategy also works well for older kids who always have pressing questions like "How does the microwave oven work?" as soon as you begin to talk on the telephone.

46
Sweet Lovin'

Purpose: To teach and encourage gentle, loving expression
To further develop verbal skills

Equipment: Any soft dolls or stuffed animals

Position: Place the baby on the floor or in her infant seat. Sit next to her. Have several dolls or stuffed animals with you.

Procedure:
1. Pick up a doll. Hug it gently and say, "Oh, I just love this doll. I'm going to give her a hug and a kiss!" Then do it.
2. Hand the doll to your baby, saying, "Do you love this doll too? Can you give her a big hug?"
3. When your baby reaches out to hold the doll, take her arms and show her how to hug the doll.
4. Ask for the doll back, saying, "Oh, I just love her so! Could I give her another hug? Don't you just love her?"

5. As the baby hands you the doll, give it some more hugs and kisses. If she is reluctant to give up the doll, go on to another doll or stuffed animal, repeating Step 1.

6. Continue showing your baby how to hug, hold, pat, or kiss the different dolls and animals you have out. Trade animals and dolls back and forth.

Variations: 1. If you want to extend the game, you can name parts of the face or body as you are hugging. "I love this doll's eyes—see her eyes, Katie?"

2. You can teach any kind of loving gestures you want. We loved little pats on the back and felt the game had really paid off when those pudgy hands gently patted our backs.

Suggestion: Be sure to hug and pat your baby (and older child) as part of the game too!

Including ore Players: This game is wonderful for an older brother or sister who needs to see that everyone needs and should get loving cuddle time! An older sister can rock or sing to a doll if bored with simple hugs.

47

Splish, Splash
A Warm Weather Game

Purpose: To have some good cool fun

Equipment: Sand bucket or unbreakable bowl, serving spoons, measuring cups, or sand shovels

Position: First, find a good spot outdoors for the baby to play Splish, Splash. Place your baby in front of a half-filled bucket of water.

Procedure: 1. Get your baby started by gently splashing her hands in the water.
2. If she enjoys it, give her a spoon or measuring cup to dip and splash with.

Variations: The possibilities for this game are endless. It can be played at the beach, in a sandbox, or at the park. You can use floating bath toys, Ping-Pong balls, or sponges to add to the fun. On a hot day, a bucket of water can be filled and spilled many times before interest in the game lags.

Suggestion: Strip the baby down to her diapers for this game.

Including More Players: A child of any age will enjoy water play. A small inflatable swimming pool is a good idea for two or more children. With only a few inches of water, even your baby can join in the cool splashing fun!

Conclusion

Your baby is a year old now! Isn't it hard to believe? Did
it go by fast? I told you so! Think back over that fir
year—such tremendous growth and amazin
discoveries—not only for your baby, but for the who
family. And aren't you glad now that you took the time
play games and learn about your baby right from the star
She may not win a gold medal at the Olympics because
it, but she *will* have learned a lot about herself, her worl
and her family.

And what about you? Remember how anxious yo
were? Concerned that you wouldn't do the right thing
the right time. Don't you feel good? It stands to reaso
After all, the better you know a person, the better you ca
anticipate her needs or understand her problems. As yo
know, we feel the best way to get to know someone is
play with her—and this book was written for those of
who aren't sure exactly what to play. So, we hope *Mo
Games Babies Play* came in handy in helping you enjo
your baby's first year.

And for those parents who had older brothers or sisters to play the games too, we hope that sharing Katie's first year of games with Amy has helped you cope with all that energy and possible jealousy. It gets easier all the time and now that the groundwork for games is laid, the best is yet to come—

Happy Birthday!

Bringing Up A Brighter, Happier Child

The growth of a child's mind is a wonderful thing to watch. And it's even more wonderful when you've read up on the subject. Pocket Books has a fine list of titles about the mental development of children written by prominent specialists in the field.

If you are a parent, or soon plan to be, you'll want these books for your home library.

_____	46840	HOW TO RAISE A BRIGHTER CHILD Joan Beck	$3.50
_____	46839	IMPROVING YOUR CHILD'S BEHAVIOR CHEMISTRY Lendon Smith, MD	$3.50
_____	45763	UNDERSTANDING YOUR CHILD FROM BIRTH TO THREE Joseph Church	$2.95

POCKET BOOKS,
Department CCB
1230 Avenue of the Americas
New York, N.Y. 10020

Please send me the books I have checked above. I am enclosing $_____ (please add 75¢ to cover postage and handling, N.Y.S. and N.Y.C. residents please add appropriate sales tax). Send check or money order—no cash or C.O.D.s please. Allow six weeks for delivery. For purchases over $10.00, you may use VISA: card number, expiration date and customer signature must be included.

NAME _____

ADDRESS _____

CITY _____ STATE/ZIP _____

653

11

NOVELS BY

ROBERT A. HEINLEIN

05500	Between Planets	95c
10600	Citizen of the Galaxy	95c
31800	Have Space Suit—Will Travel	95c
71140	Red Planet	95c
73330	Rocket Ship Galileo	95c
73440	The Rolling Stones	95c
77730	Space Cadet	95c
78000	The Star Beast	95c
81125	Time for the Stars	95c
82660	Tunnel in the Sky	95c
91501	The Worlds of Robert A. Heinlein	60c

EDGAR RICE BURROUGHS

Gothics galore from ace books
MARGARET ERSKINE

Don't miss these exciting adventures of Peacelord of the Universe!
PERRY RHODAN

━━ ━━━━━━━━━━ ━━ ━━ ━━━━━━━━ ━━ ━━ ━━━━━━━━ ━